Remembrance and Reflection

50 years on: The Birmingham Bombings

Copyright ©2024 Maggie Fogarty

Maggie Fogarty has asserted the right to be identified as the publisher and compiler of this book in accordance with the Copyright Designs and Patents Act 1988

No part of this publication may be reproduced, stored in or introduced into a retrieval system, or transmitted, in any form, or by any means (electronic, mechanical, photocopying, recording or otherwise) without the written permission of the publisher except that brief selections may be quoted or copied without permission, provided that full credit is given.

FOREWORD

Having arrived as a history lecturer at the University of Birmingham in 2010, I first became aware of the enduring impacts of the pub bombings amid events to commemorate the 40th anniversary in 2014. As a scholar of racism, I was interested in the anti-Irish violence that occurred in the aftermath of the bombings and its long-term impacts on Birmingham's Irish community. I remember being shocked at the twenty-one-year absence of the St Patrick's Day Parade, and by stories of people masking accents and hiding ethnic identities.

With my colleague Saima Nasar, I decided to put on a 'witness seminar' at the University to record some testimony for posterity, inviting Julie Hambleton alongside members of the emergency services and a representative of the Irish community (Rick Sinclair from the local Irish Heritage Group). Many important stories were told on that night but what emerged most clearly, from the audience as well as the contributors, was a feeling that Birmingham had never found sufficient space to commemorate the pub bombings. Aside from the dignified but small memorial in St Philip's Square, little had been done in the city to mark what was a catastrophic night in Birmingham's history, and so a group of us set out to change that.

At first, it was hard to convince the Irish community to play much of a role. Several local leaders and activists made it clear to us that they thought those dark events were best left in the past, but Maurice Malone, whose painful personal story is told in this important new collection, took a different view. Working with Saima and myself, with Maureen Slattery Marsh from ICAP, Rick Sinclair and Julie Hambleton, Maurice led the Misneach Memorial Committee to establish a new city centre memorial, now known as the Tree Memorial, which was finished in 2018. Through this act of memorialisation, the Irish community and the families of the victims came together in a way which highlighted both the hurt that was long felt by both, but also the generous spirit and open-hearted nature of all involved. In his testimony below, Alfred White explains that 'trauma can divide communities but it can also bring us together'. Over the last ten years, I have been privileged to witness the truth of this statement first hand.

Reconciliation and remembrance grow on foundations of truth and justice. As Breda Power's story here reminds us, the aftermath of the pub bombings witnessed the very opposite in Birmingham, with the prosecution and imprisonment of the Birmingham Six, and the broader vilification of innocent Irish people, many of whom were forced from their jobs and left feeling unsafe in their homes. The real perpetrators of the pub bombings have never been held to account for their crimes, nor at this stage are they likely to be. Nonetheless, by listening to those who were for many years ignored and by creating space for victims to tell and record their stories, the impact of the Birmingham pub bombings and all that came after can come to the fore.

These stories are nothing less than the roots of Birmingham's history, which is why a collection such as this is so vitally important. Over the years, it has been my greatest privilege to work with the victims and their families and witness their dignity, resilience and kindness. On this 50th anniversary, I am proud to stand with them and all the people of Birmingham as we remember what was lost on that night and work together to heal the many wounds that remain, fifty years on.

Gavin Schaffer

Professor of Modern British History

Manchester Metropolitan University

INTRODUCTION

Back in 2004 I produced the BBC documentary '30 Years On: The Birmingham Bombings' written and presented by the respected journalist David Jessel. The programme featured the stories of survivors of the IRA bombings which exploded in two packed city centre pubs on November 21st 1974 killing 21 people and injuring around 200 others. We also heard from police officers who were first on the scene; covered the conviction and release of the 'Birmingham Six'; and interviewed members of the Birmingham Irish community past and present.

While as a production team we were proud of the programme – it went on to get a Royal Television Society (Midlands) award – the stories had to be told within the confines of a half hour transmission slot.

Fast forward twenty years and I have moved on from being a TV producer, returning to my working roots as a print journalist/writer.

The idea for this commemorative book first came as I met with some fellow writers and organisers of the 2023 Authorcity Birmingham event.

We were meeting at a venue overlooking the city's St Philip's Cathedral, where the original modest memorial stone to the 21 people killed stands. At one point our talk turned to the subject of the forthcoming 50th anniversary of the tragedy and the impact of that terrible event on the city.

An early thought was to produce a book of short stories, a creative tribute rather than a factual one. However, the idea of returning to the original TV programme contributors - allowing for more detail and nuance with some additional voices - won the day.

Of course I knew that a few of the people featured in the documentary had passed away. Also would any of the others want to return to the subject two decades later?

My first 'sounding board' was survivor Maureen Mitchell who almost died from her injuries sustained at the Mulberry Bush pub that night. She was given the last rites and was told that if she had been older – she was just 21 at the time – she probably wouldn't have made it.

After giving it some thought her answer was yes, especially as this is likely to be the last 'big' anniversary before the tragic event starts to fade from living memory. Maureen was also taken with the idea of being part of a commemorative book which she could pass on to other members of her family, a lasting testimony to what she had gone through and the longer term impact on her life.

Other contributors felt the same including former police officer Margaret Adams, who was one of the first on the scene at the Mulberry Bush and afterwards had the poignant task of returning personal items from the dead and injured to their relatives. Likewise former police officer John Plimmer, who along with a colleague, escaped death by minutes – they had visited the second bombed pub, the Tavern in the Town, shortly before the explosion.

On the basis of these conversations, I decided to go ahead, retelling their stories with a mix of interviews and pieces written by themselves. There are also some new voices added, people who didn't appear in the TV documentary but whose stories came to my attention afterwards.

One of these is senior psychiatrist, Dr Alfred White, who was involved in some important early research into the mental health impact of the bombings on the lesser injured survivors.

A lot has happened in the intervening 20 years including the 2019 inquest into the deaths of the 21 people who lost their lives that night, ruling that they were unlawfully killed.

During the Inquest - held 45 years after the bombings and successfully campaigned for by Justice4the21 group and the Birmingham Mail newspaper - 'Witness O' named four men as responsible for the bombings, saying that he had been given permission to name them by the then head of the IRA in Dublin.

Meantime the Justice4the21 campaign, founded by Julie and Brian Hambleton, whose sister Maxine died in the Tavern in the Town bombing, is demanding a full statutory public inquiry into the bombings. Their campaign is a bigger separate story which is still unfolding and will be told elsewhere.

Fifty years on there remains an enduring sense that justice has not been served for the people killed, the bereaved families, and those left with life changing injuries.

The inter-generational trauma continues to this day and the voices featured here give their own personal accounts on the lasting effects of those terrible events. In spite of this, there are stories of triumph over adversity despite the physical and mental scars.

As a teenager at the time, studying for exams and from a working class Birmingham Irish Catholic background, I remember only too well the backlash against the wider Irish community which continued for some years afterwards. I vividly recall my mum saying the day after the bombings that she felt 'ashamed' to be Irish which at the time I couldn't understand – after all it wasn't us who had committed the crimes. Sadly in the eyes of a small but vocal number, just by having an Irish name or accent meant that our community was tainted by association. I wish I could say that wouldn't happen today but recent events show that misdirected anger against a number of communities still exists.

Thankfully the Irish community in the city emerged from this dark time showing the same steeliness and resilience as the wider Birmingham community. The beautiful metal 'tree' tribute which stands outside Birmingham's Grand Central (New Street) railway station, displaying the names of the 21 people who died that night, was made possible by the Birmingham Irish Association working alongside the families of the bereaved. It is an enduring symbol of the city's strength against those who brought carnage and death just a short walk away, with its message of hope over adversity.

'The Leaves Of The Tree Are For the Healing Of The Nations'.

Maggie Fogarty

MAUREEN MITCHELL'S STORY

The night of the bombings...

The evening of November 21st 1974 started like most Thursday evenings. At the time I was a 21 year old, engaged to be married and looking forward to meeting my fiancé Ian Lord at our usual drinking haunt – the Mulberry Bush pub, right next to Birmingham's iconic Rotunda building.

The pub was only a short walk from my bus stop in Corporation Street and as we made our way to the pub, the streets were busy with late-night shoppers. Back then Thursday was payday for a lot of people and a good number of shops were open later than usual in the run-up to Christmas. Apart from the festive atmosphere this could have been any Thursday night, the weekend looming and a fresh pay packet.

When we got to the Mulberry Bush around 7.30 pm we struck up a conversation with our friend Stan Bodman, a regular at the pub. He was standing by a rear door which led out towards New Street station. Ian was a friend of Stan's sons - they'd been to the same school and had played football together. I can't recall what we talked about but I do remember Stan inviting us to join him for a drink. We declined because I was keen to chat to Ian privately about something, so we moved to a table further into the pub just by the stairway leading to the upper floor.

Little did we know how important that small decision would

turn out to be. I wasn't looking forward to telling Ian that he couldn't come along to my works Christmas party.

The Christmas party was for employees only, with no family members, spouses or other partners invited. Ian was listening but didn't have time to reply. As the words came out of my mouth, our lives were about to be shattered.

Just before the bombs went off a warning call was made to the local newspaper office by a man with an Irish accent. He gave a special code to show he was genuine and said that bombs had been planted at the tax office in New Street and at the Rotunda. Minutes later the two bombs exploded. Except it wasn't the Rotunda or the tax office, but two busy nearby pubs full of people, chatting and drinking with friends.

I remember being thrown across the room, feeling that my tights were being torn from my legs. There was a lot of screaming and above this I could hear Ian calling out to me. My legs were trapped and eventually Ian found me, pulling off pieces of wood and debris. With the help of a security man from the nearby Rotunda building, I was taken outside and laid out on the ground next to a wall at New Street station. I knew I had hurt my leg but at that stage couldn't feel pain anywhere else.

It seemed like a lifetime before the emergency vehicles arrived though in reality it was quite quick. Ian managed to get me into one of the first ambulances on the scene and I remember a man lying next to me with his face in a terrible state and me thinking 'poor man'.

While I was making my way to the General Hospital, Ian stayed put to see if he could get back inside the pub to find Stan. Despite his own injuries – a perforated eardrum, a cut to his leg and a face injury - he managed to make his way in and all he could see was a pile of rubble where our friend had been standing.

When I got to the General hospital I realised that I'd injured my stomach as well and by now was in severe pain. I remember begging for more pain killers but was told that they couldn't give me a higher dose until they had assessed my 'head injury' – the first time I heard about it. In the end I found out that fragments of metal had entered my bowel, I had leg and head injuries and a bad deep upper arm burn caused by molten plastic. At one point over the coming hours I was so ill that I had to be given the last rites.

Ten people who were in the Mulberry Bush pub died that night and a further eleven who were in another popular pub, The Tavern in the Town, just up the road in New Street. Some 200 others were hurt, a number of them with life-changing injuries. Bombs had been placed in both pubs and our lives and home city of Birmingham were changed forever.

It took a while for my mum and dad to find out where I was as we didn't have a telephone at home and they had to use a local telephone box. Eventually they got through to Ian's parents to find out what had happened and rushed to the hospital in the early hours. In the chaos they were taken to see another badly injured young woman who my mum realised straight away wasn't me. In his shocked state, dad was convinced that it was me and mum told me afterwards that he would have believed anyone was his daughter just for the assurance that I was still alive. When they did get to see me I was fighting for my life with a strong chance that I wouldn't pull through. Ian was at another hospital being treated for his injuries along with so many others across the city.

What started out as an ordinary Thursday night out turned into a nightmare, with 21 people never waking up. I could easily have been one of those but with the help of Ian, a security guard, the medical staff and my young level of physical fitness I managed, against all the odds, to pull through.

Sadly our friend Stan didn't survive.

My life before the bombings

Some of those killed and injured, including myself, had an Irish family background. Birmingham had been a magnet for Irish people after the Second World War with a high demand for workers and the chance to make a better living. My dad, Jim Carlin, was one of those who made the journey across the water from Derry in the late 1940s in search of work. He soon met my mum Cynthia, who was born in Birmingham, and they set up home in the Bartley Green area of the city.

I came along in 1953, the middle one of five children, two girls and three boys. Dad worked in the car industry and mum took on a number of jobs to fit around the family including cleaning work.

Growing up, we were aware of our Irish side of the family and I remember getting bunches of shamrock in the post from relatives in Ireland for St Patrick's Day. I went to a local Catholic primary school and proudly wore a little sprig of the shamrock pinned to my school jumper.

I left school at 15 and joined my older sister working in a clerical job at a finance company. With my own money to spend, I started going out to various night clubs in the city centre with my best friend Carmel. There were no age checks back then and I remember putting on make-up during the bus journey there and then wiping it off before I got home as my mum didn't approve of me wearing it. During the late 1960s, I became aware of the growing 'troubles' in Northern Ireland but we didn't talk much about that at home. Looking back I wish I had spoken more to my dad about the situation but as a teenager I was more concerned about music and going out with friends. In fact when I was 16, I travelled on my own over to Derry to visit my grandmother, going by train and ferry. An older cousin took me to a dance at Culdaff Marquee and this was when the 'troubles' had worsened, with night-time curfews and soldiers stationed all over the place. I remember us laughing and showing our dance tickets to the young soldiers, many of them with English accents. I was also in Derry on July 12 1969 which is the day of all the big 'Orange' protestant loyalist parades. There was tension in the air but as a carefree teenager it didn't bother me too much. If anything it felt quite exciting, away from home on my own.

By 1974 I was working at a city centre advertising agency and I loved it there, dealing with all the client bookings. I was also engaged to my first serious boyfriend, Ian and we had our wedding planned for June 1975 with my friend Carmel as one of the bridesmaids.

It was a carefree and exciting time. Until bombers struck right in the heart of the city. When my dad went back into work after the atrocity, he was met with anger on the factory floor and reviled for having an Irish accent. Then they discovered that I was fighting for my life at the General Hospital. After that he was left alone.

For years he kept the battered umbrella I was carrying that night, along with the coat I was wearing, in our garden shed. Maybe this was his own small way of acknowledging how lucky I was to survive.

Life after the bombings

I was in the General Hospital for 4 weeks and got out just before Christmas. I was still in pain from the injuries and had to attend hospital over the coming months to treat my burns. I returned to work in February 1975 and was bowled over by the many get well cards and gifts I received from complete strangers who were horrified by what had happened. My dad didn't want us to go ahead with the wedding so soon after the trauma of the bombings. He thought I should give myself more time to recover after almost losing my life but we were determined to stick to our plans, to show the bombers that they hadn't won. The wedding had already been booked and we had a great day celebrating with family and friends.

Afterwards we settled into married life and I continued to work at the agency. When the Mulberry Bush pub re-opened, I decided not to go along to the opening night with Ian as I just wasn't ready. Eventually I did go back in with some friends who were a bit concerned about how it would affect me but it was something I had to do - again to prove that those who planted the bombs hadn't won. Strangely enough, entering the place where I almost lost my life wasn't as bad as I thought it would be and over the years I continued to go back in there.

I was approaching my thirties when I became pregnant with my son, who we also called Ian. This was 8 years after we got married and though I had physically recovered from my injuries, I was worried that the scarring from my stomach wounds might interfere with me having a baby. The doctors said that the only way to know would be to try and the pregnancy went well thankfully.

Before my son started school I did a few part-time jobs and afterwards became a home care worker with Birmingham social services department, visiting older residents in their homes.

Eventually I moved across to the administrative side of things, working in the home care office. While there I was approached by the Lord Mayor's office about a new reconciliation project called LIVE (Let's Involve the Victims Experience) set up in Dublin to introduce families from across the UK and Irish Republic whose lives had been impacted by terrorism attacks. This was in 2000 and I felt that by sharing my own experiences with others, it might help me to understand more about what had happened in my home city.

Taking part in the reconciliation project involved flying out to Dublin every few weeks on a Friday evening and meeting at a remote venue in the Wicklow Mountains. Despite the name of the project, we were encouraged to see ourselves as 'survivors' and not 'victims'.

It was here that I met Colin Parry who lost his 12 year old son Tim in the 1993 Warrington bombings, when two bombs exploded in a crowded shopping area of the town. Alongside his wife Wendy, Colin founded the Tim Parry and Johnathan Ball Foundation as a living memorial to his son and three year old Johnathan, who was also killed by the IRA bomb in Warrington. They work with schools, communities, police and local authorities, to resolve conflict through dialogue and conflict resolution techniques. The idea is to use early intervention and prevention to help stop violence before it starts.

Getting involved in the reconciliation project was a sort of therapy for me and I spoke to a number of people whose lives had been changed forever by terrorism. I met the parents of the last British soldier who was killed before the Good Friday Agreement was signed on 10 April 1998, effectively bringing to an end three decades of conflict known as the Troubles. It was good to share our experiences and we all got to know each other's personal stories of violent attacks and the lasting effects.

Later on we were asked how we would feel about meeting 'ex-combatants' as they were called, people who had gone to prison for committing terrorist related attacks and had been released as part of the Good Friday Agreement. Some of those taking part refused to meet them but I decided that I would do. I needed to try to process why someone could go into a busy pub full of young people enjoying themselves and plant a bomb.

For me it was all about trying to get some kind of insight, not to in any shape or form to excuse their actions which I could never do. The first time the ex-combatants arrived, we were asked to choose someone speak to. After I got talking to one of the men we ended up going outside for a walk at about 10pm at night. I just kept thinking, here I am in the middle of nowhere talking to someone I've only just met and know little about their past. It was surreal.

We just talked about his early life, how he got involved in violence as a young man and how easy it was to get drawn into things. By the end of the weekend, I found myself feeling sad for the youngster that he once was. My husband joined one group session speaking to another of the combatants released after the Good Friday Agreement. After he left prison he changed his life completely and if you didn't know about his violent past you would never have believed it. You he told a shocking story about how he would walk his children to church, saying hello to the priest while he had hidden guns inside the children's coats. He was one of the few who did say that he regretted what he had done in the past. Others said that they wouldn't do it now but sadly there was no apology for past actions.

I was left thinking that if I'd been brought up in that

environment, had we gone to live in my dad's birthplace in Derry, could I have got caught up in that way of thinking? I'm not saying it was right what they did but it must be difficult for young people when you are under pressure to take part in things from members of your own family.

I did miss the LIVE resolution meetings after they stopped, especially the other survivors who took part. We had all got to know one another and it was a bit like a bereavement when we finished - there had been such a shared bond between us and the emotions connected with it. We spoke about our innermost feelings at the toughest times in our lives but as odd as it sounds, there was laughter and humour too. When I listened to some of the other stories I thought that what I had gone through wasn't so bad.

After meeting Colin and Wendy Parry, I used to go up occasionally to the foundation peace centre in Warrington. I would take part in story telling sessions where I described what happened to me and the idea was to encourage conflict resolution as opposed to violence.

Again most of the people in the group had been involved in some sort of atrocity whether it was being injured or bereaved from a terror attack. There were also parents of soldiers who had been killed or injured whilst serving in Northern Ireland.

During the sessions at Warrington we shared stories about our feelings and emotions, while also looking at ways to help us deal with it all. Some of us went on to complete a Peer Support accreditation to try and help others come to terms with what had happened to them

I recall a sibling of one of the soldiers who died, talking about how he felt forgotten as his parents dealt with their loss even though he was grieving too. I think it is sometimes easy to forget that whatever happened to us had a knock on effect to others around us.

We also met some wonderful people who we would not have had the opportunity to meet if these things had not happened to us - people like Mo Mowlam, John Major and Bobby Charlton.

My mum and dad had already passed away when I got involved with the LIVE project. Looking back, I wished that I had taken more of an interest about the Northern Ireland situation when I was growing up. My mum would probably have disapproved of me taking part in the project but I'm not sure how my dad who have felt.

A memorable occasion was when I was asked to take part in a talk with MPs at the House of Commons. I was terrified about speaking to them but Colin Parry advised me just to keep looking over at him while I did it. The talk was about Colin and Wendy's resolution work and how I had got involved in this area. Afterwards I felt proud to have done the talk, to stand up in front of all those MPs and tell my story.

I'm no longer involved in reconciliation work but whenever there are terrorist attacks, like the Manchester arena bombing, it brings back the memories of fifty years ago. My husband Andy said to me recently that he thought it did me good to take part in the reconciliation project. He said I seemed a lot calmer afterwards.

As for my own extended Irish family, we lost touch when my dad and older brother died. It's what often happens, after the older generation pass away.

Who knows whether that will change again over the coming years?

Reflecting on my life today

People have often asked me how being a survivor of the Birmingham bombings has changed my life, not just physically but mentally.

Of course physically I still have the scars, with a large visible mark on my upper arm where I got burned from molten plastic. I have got used to that now and it is just part of who I am. Despite my mum telling me after I got out of hospital that I should get rid of my halter neck tops and sleeveless blouses because 'you won't be able to wear those now', I don't hide my scar.

Although being close to death that night, my health has been generally good and I've always had the determination not to let what happened destroy my life. That has been my personal win and my way of dealing with it.

Today there is a lot more help for people involved in tragedies than there was back in 1974. Fifty years ago we were fixed medically but then just expected to go back to where things were – after I started to recover physically my mum would say, 'come on Maureen it is time to get back to work'. That's just how it was back then and it wouldn't happen today with people having more help with the mental health side of things

While I've coped by getting on with life, things have not always been easy. There have been dark times over the years and there is still the psychological wound that justice has not been served, that it may never happen after so many years. I've also been through a divorce which is never easy. I am now happily remarried, have my grandchildren who are a complete joy and feel that life has been good to me in so many ways. It could have been very different if I had let what happened define me.

Today I am retired and able to spend time with my family and grandchildren. Who knows what my life would have been like if I hadn't been at the Mulberry Bush on the evening of November 21st 1974? All I know is that 'there but the grace' and I might not have survived. Although this was a long time ago, people's memories are still raw in Birmingham. My older granddaughter was doing something about the Second World War at school and heard about how the city was bombed. This then got us talking about my own experience of bombings many years later. It is part of the city's history and is important that younger generations know what happened.

My simple message to any younger people reading this is that hopefully you will never have to face such an atrocity in your young lives but do try to see the wider picture of how and why these events come about.

On the 50th anniversary of the bombings I will be at Birmingham Cathedral, as I have been over the years, to remember those who died and the others whose lives were shattered that night. The anniversary will fall on a Thursday just as it was half a century ago in a different world. Near the wall where I lay critically injured there is the beautiful steel tree memorial feature, each of the 21 'leaves' bearing the names of all those who died just a short distance away. A place where people can go to remember and reflect in the shadow of the two former pubs.

IAN LORD'S STORY

After Maureen was put into the ambulance I made my way back into the pub to look for our friend Stan. I had injuries to my face and leg and found out afterwards that I had a perforated ear drum. When I got to the serving hatch where Stan had been drinking there was just a big pile of rubble.

While waiting outside for an ambulance I remember saying to a man that I could do with a cigarette and him telling me that he didn't know how I could smoke it 'with that hole in your face'. My cheek had an open wound and when I arrived at the Accident Hospital there was blood everywhere. A woman was staring across at me horrified at the state of my face and I then realised what a mess I must look. When I left the hospital two weeks later, I went straight away to visit Maureen and then for a pint with my dad – I wanted to get straight back to doing something normal and that included going into a pub. When the Mulberry Bush pub reopened I was there as well.

Of course I was angry about what happened, with Maureen seriously injured and our friend Stan one of the dead. I had an Irish friend who wanted to visit Maureen in hospital and when he arrived to see her he was worried that I wouldn't want him there because he was Irish. I wasn't angry with him and in fact some of the nurses who treated me in hospital were also Irish. I didn't agree with the backlash against some of the Irish community at the time and Maureen's dad came from Ireland as well.

Our wedding was the main focus afterwards and when Maureen came out of hospital we decided just to get on with our lives, to stick to our plans. We had a good wedding day and if we had changed the date, the bombers would have won. I still go to the Cathedral service on November 21st each year to remember those who died including our friend Stan. The impact of the bombings is felt in the city to this day by the families and friends of those killed and injured. That's why it is important for people to keep remembering what happened that night and to commemorate the 21 lives lost.

STANLEY BODMAN TRIBUTE

Stanley 'Stan' Bodman, a regular at the Mulberry Bush, was among a group of friends who were killed while standing at the bar of the pub on November 21st 1974.

Stan, a 47-year-old electrician who worked in the city centre, was there with Michael Beasley, John Rowlands, Cliff Jones and James Caddick.

His son Paul Bodman gave a moving portrait of his father at the 2019 inquests, as did other family members of the 21 victims.

He said: "The carnage of that night will never be forgotten" adding that the family hoped the inquest would finally bring some answers to "what really happened on that devastating night".

Paul said the family remembered their father, a former RAF serviceman, as the "funniest and kindest person anyone could ever wish to meet".

He told the inquest the family regularly talked about the risk of a pub bombing because of warnings at the time and added that as ex-RAF his father was "fully aware of the devastation a bomb could do".

Paul said: "He would always reassure me there was no need to worry, because I used to drink in there regularly with him, because the targets in those days were thought to be political or military targets, not public.

"So we weren't expecting anything to happen like that in the pubs. We certainly got that wrong."

Paul described father of three Stan as a "larger than life personality" and "very popular" - adding that he never missed a day's work, and those who knew him said he had "an easy charm and a slight air of mystery".

Also that he was a "lovely, quiet man" and a "gentleman, mild-mannered and agreeable", always known for being well-dressed.

Paul told how his father had a great love of sport, especially boxing and cricket, and spent time at Edgbaston watching Warwickshire.

"He was one of the funniest and kindest people anyone could ever wish to meet and he was taken away from his family far too soon," he said.

Just two weeks before the bombings the Bodman family had met up at the Mulberry Bush.

Paul said: "Who would have thought that it would be the last time our family would get together in full?"

CAROL PEARCE'S STORY

On November 21st 1974, Carol Eaglesfield as she was called back then, was an 18 year old trainee manager at Etam clothing shop on New Street.

She remembers being warned that day to look out for any suspicious packages – everyone was on high alert due to the big police operation around the body of IRA activist James McDade being flown back to Ireland.

'As a typical 18 year old I wasn't too bothered by it and when my friend Heather suggested that we go for a drink after work at the nearby Tavern In The Town pub I was happy to go,' Carol recalls.

They had just sat down with their drinks when they heard a massive rumbling sound and wondered what on earth it was.

At the time they were sitting by a post with seating alcoves on either side of them and as usual the pub was busy. Within minutes there was a massive explosion inside the pub, killing the barman who had served them and all the people sitting nearby.

'I'm still not sure to this day how myself and Heather survived,' Carol says. She says that before being rescued from the damaged pub, God told her that she had survived for a reason and that was to do work for the local community.

Afterwards, she and her friend were helped outside covered in debris and were taken to a hotel across the road in New Street to wait for transport to hospital. She recalls seeing a young police officer sobbing.

Carol had extensive burns on her legs where her trousers and tights had stuck to her skin. Her left ear drum was punctured leaving her with long term hearing loss and tinnitus. She also had an L shaped wound on her back and her friend Heather had facial injuries.

She was taken to the General Hospital by taxi and she describes the drivers as heroes that night as the ambulances struggled to deal with the number of injured people. Miraculously she had found her handbag and managed to find the phone number of her aunt who had a home telephone. Like many others at that time, her parents didn't have one.

Her aunt and uncle collected her parents and they arrived at the hospital past midnight.

'When they got there I was about to go into the operating theatre and was confused, unable to hear properly but at least they knew I had survived.'

'The atmosphere was chaotic and after mum and dad got back home exhausted in the early hours, they had a visit from a police officer to inform them that I was in hospital.'

'For a terrible moment they thought he had come to tell them that I had died of my injuries.'

'When I came out of the operating theatre I was given a special skin protective cover and they thought that I might need skin grafts. I kept telling them that I couldn't hear properly and as it turned out, both of my eardrums had been damaged.'

'After two weeks in hospital, I left in a wheelchair and needed months of physiotherapy on my legs. I was living in my parents' flat at the top of three flights of stairs with no lift. As my walking improved, I was taken to hospital and back two or three times each week by a Mr Scarff of the Round Table Charity.'

'My dad in particular was furious after the bombings, saying that he had gone through the war unscathed only to have his daughter badly injured in supposed peacetime. My mum was devastated too and had to help me with basic things like going to the toilet.'

'I was on Valium for a year and barely went out. Three months after the bombings my dad suggested that it might be good to confront my fear and re-visit the scene. My cousin John was one of the people working on clearing the debris at the Tavern pub and I plucked up the courage to go back down the stairs and saw the extent of the carnage. I think it did help and then a year later I had an ear operation to replace my left ear drum.'

Despite all of this Carol considers herself lucky and a year after the bombings she met her husband Roy Pearce when he was best man and she was a bridesmaid at a friend's wedding.

They married in 1977 and press photographers turned up to cover the story of the young Carol finding happiness after surviving the bombings. Due to the press coverage, their own wedding photographer got delayed and by the time they got to their reception venue the caterers had started to pack away the food. Fortunately the reception went ahead and the couple are still together with three children of their own and are now grandparents.

Carol never did return to her retail work even though they kept her job open. Instead she fulfilled the promise she made to herself when she sat waiting to be taken to hospital, knowing she had survived but unsure about how badly injured she was.

'I'd always had a Christian faith and what happened that night changed my life in a good way too. I decided to get involved in working with young people in the community, running the Red Welly Youth Club with my husband Roy and then getting involved in community projects like the Green Apple Crafts Project'

She also did a secretarial course and then went to work at the National Trust Back to Backs project featuring the city's last surviving court of back-to-back houses. In 2017 she left the project but is still actively involved in community work both through the church and is chair of the Yardley Conservation Society, which works to preserve older buildings and landmarks in that part of the city.

Reflecting on her life today Carol says:

'I know it was a terrible night with so many innocent people losing their lives but I personally don't feel bitter. Although I still have health problems with tinnitus and nerve damage to my ears, I've also had a long and happy marriage, a family and got involved in fulfilling community work. While I will never forget what happened, my Christian faith has allowed me to appreciate what I have in my life and to move forward.'

LEE BENSON'S STORY

On the night of November 21st 1974 I was in the city centre celebrating with my friend Stuart who had just passed his driving test the day before.

I was living at my parents' house in Moseley at the time and had cheerfully told my mum that we were heading out to the Mulberry Bush pub. We liked it and there was always a good crowd, including a group we called the 'Rackham's Girls' – they used to go in after they finished work at the nearby department store. It was about 6.30pm when we arrived and the place was already busy.

Then we made a decision which was likely to have saved our lives. At about 7.35pm we decided to head over to a place in Moseley to get some fish and chips, with newly qualified driver Stuart taking us there in his dad's car.

While we were chatting and eating our meal we knew nothing about the bombs that had just gone off in two pubs in the city centre – one of them in the Mulberry Bush where we had been less than an hour before.

It was around 9.15pm when I arrived home and I'll never forget the sight that greeted me. My mum was lying on the floor screaming uncontrollably, with dad trying to comfort her. She had heard the news about the bombings and knew that myself and Stuart were going to the Mulberry Bush pub. With no mobile phones or any other way to get in touch, she hadn't heard from us and thought we were dead or injured.

That image of my mum has remained with me all these years and it was only after I got home that I learned what had happened. A couple of years ago I met up with Stuart again and while we were sitting at a bar in Tel Aviv I said to him that we could have had our lives ended or changed forever that night. We might easily have stayed put at the Mulberry Bush but for some reason we didn't.

Since then I have had a fear of going into crowded places, triggered by the images of me and my friend in that busy Birmingham pub about an hour before the bomb went off. Four decades later I was persuaded by my wife to go to the Isle of Wight see the group Fleetwood Mac and confronted my fear by positioning ourselves in front of the camera and film gantry. It meant we had a very safe area and I didn't have to be right inside the 78,000 audience. That's the strange thing – I have played in bands in front of crowds and I am OK with that as long as I'm not in there amongst them.

My mum, who died a few years ago, was born in Dublin and my dad was Jewish. Fortunately she didn't suffer any abuse after the bombings - she was a small but fierce Irish woman and wouldn't have put up with any of that.

Only a month before the pub bombings, a car belonging to the wife of the then Labour government environment minister, Denis Howell, was targeted outside their family home which backed onto our street. The noise was horrendous and I remember looking out of my bedroom window terrified. A bomb had been planted under their car by the IRA. Fortunately no one was killed but that was all to change just few weeks later with the bombs in the city centre.

To this day I can't stand the noise of fireworks, it reminds me of the car bomb going off near our house - and when I visit

London I have to avoid crowded tube trains. In July 2005 I thought both my daughters had been caught up in the London transport bombings – they were due to travel on the bus that was targeted – but fortunately they ended up missing it. Events like this trigger my memories of the Birmingham bombings which still surface all these decades later.

The bombings changed Birmingham back then and the attitude towards the big Irish community in the city. The Irish had done so much for Birmingham – helping to rebuild it after the war, their nurses working in the hospitals, working for the car industry and a whole host of other jobs – only to get blamed by some for what happened.

All that has changed over the years but it is still important to remember what happened that night, with the real and lasting consequences. In my case I have had to learn to live with my persistent fear of crowded places and the image of my mum screaming on the floor when she thought her son had been killed or seriously injured. That awful scene will stay with me forever.

MARGARET ADAMS' STORY

As I'm writing this, the memories from fifty years ago are still there as if it was only last month. Strange as it might sound, I particularly remember a handbag which was retrieved from one of the bombed pubs. Although dirty on the outside, its contents inside were relatively undamaged, and we were able to trace the owner who had sadly died in the bombing.

I visited her family. I think she was 17 or 18 and had worked in town and stopped after work to socialise in the pub with her friends. Her parents were lovely and so grateful to receive it and I sat in their home with them, their sadness palpable.

It was a humbling experience.

Before this tragedy in November 1974, I was a young policewoman working in the heart of the city, on general police duties. I loved my work being involved with people in the community and feeling with the confidence of the young that I could make a real difference.

I had moved from Thames Valley Police working in a rural area, to work in the city and to marry my husband who was also a servicing police officer. We had met at Police Training College near Coventry two years earlier and decided to make Birmingham our home. He was on duty that night too, working in a different area. We had just bought our first house and we were happy, keen and enthusiastic about our work.

At the time I was working with several other women in the

then Policewomen's Department which meant specifically working with women and children. We did shift work, early 8am-4pm, late 2pm-10pm, and working with the men when required on general patrol duties. As women police officers we were needed on nights every six weeks or so covering the whole of the city. There were just two of us, charging around, assisting with females who had been arrested and needed searching. We also interviewed women who had been assaulted or who were victims of rape. It was usually very busy, but again, I felt energised and keen to be working all over the city.

On 21st November 1974 all police leave was cancelled and I was scheduled to work a 2pm-10pm shift on uniform patrol working from Digbeth Police Station. Leave had been cancelled following the death of James McDade. He was a member of the IRA and was killed in a premature explosion as he was planting a bomb in Coventry a week before.

McDade's body was to be escorted back to Ireland for a funeral and this caused a great deal of tension in the city. The Archbishop of Birmingham, George Dwyer, had forbidden the paramilitary guard of honour that the Republican movement in England had planned and his body was to be flown back to Ireland for this to take place.

My shift had begun at 2pm and I had been teamed up with a uniformed male officer to patrol the city centre on the Digbeth side, as the force was on high alert, from threats from the IRA.

It was such a strange atmosphere in the station and indeed all over the city. I had never experienced anything like it. There had been several smaller explosions in Birmingham targeting symbolically important buildings and in July 1974 the Rotunda building in the heart of the city had been targeted, causing damage but no injuries. The Rotunda is still standing today but as the years have flown past there are many other high offices and shops around it and it is not the significant building it was in 1974. When I talk to my teenager grandchildren they have no idea where the Rotunda is!

Also of course there were many malicious false alarm calls, when we had had to evacuate shops or buildings, often because someone wanted a few hours off work or just to cause disruption.

I think it's important at this stage to try and imagine how different things were in 1974 particularly with regard to communication. It was so much slower. No mobile phones, no internet, no world wide web. Even my own parents didn't have a house phone, and lived two hours away. Communication was usually by letter which took two or three days. Obviously the police stations had telephones and as a young policewoman I carried a radio, almost the size of a house brick, while on patrol. But reception was poor and often non-existent.

Incidents were reported first to the central force control room and this was then conveyed to the particular area that covered the incident. All of this took several minutes, not seconds as happens today.

On the 21st of November 1974 an official warning of the bomb which had been planted was sent to the Birmingham newspaper offices using a recognised code word. By the time the message had filtered down to us on patrol in the area a precious six minutes had been lost. We received the call on our radio and we were told that a bomb had been planted in the Rotunda building.

My colleague and I were driving very close to the building and immediately responded to the call. We pulled up directly outside the entrance of the Rotunda with the intention of searching for the bomb in order that it could be de-fused, as had happened previously in other areas of the city

We arrived just before 8.20pm followed by several other officers and went into the building. As we entered the lift we felt and heard the explosion beneath us and ran outside quickly. I remember hearing a uniformed sergeant shouting "it's the "f...ing Mulberry Bush" (the pub under the Rotunda). I was shocked that he had sworn as it was forbidden to swear on the radio and it flashed through my mind that this must be really serious.

There was a small eating house next to the Rotunda and we had to evacuate that very quickly, before carrying on around the corner to the base of the Rotunda where a scene of carnage awaited us. The front of the Mulberry Bush pub had been blown out and looked like a building site. We all started to help those that were obviously wounded and some who were wandering round dazed. And my colleague rushed in through the rubble to rescue the injured inside.

Actual conversations still flow through my mind "Maggie don't come inside, they think there's another bomb" shouted at me by my work partner as he handed over a badly injured young woman he had dug from the wreckage. "Put her by the wall and stay there yourself".

I didn't of course, I made her as comfortable as possible on the ground and told a dazed young man nearby to put his arms around her and talk to her, while the ambulances arrived. I discovered afterwards, with sadness, that with the blast of the bomb she was probably deaf but I chose to think that she was comforted by someone being close to her with their arms around her, until she was taken to hospital.

Being in the city centre the ambulances arrived quickly, and taxi drivers made themselves makeshift ambulances and began to ferry the injured to hospital. A dazed man walked up to me with a severe open injury to his wrist, where his hand was hanging off. We had to almost force him into an ambulance, as he thought he wasn't injured!

For me going right inside the building with rubble, glass and timbers everywhere would have been impossible without getting injured myself. The clothing I was wearing as a police officer, flimsy shoes and nylon stockings and a straight skirt were totally impractical. Certainly rather different from the protective boots and thick trousers worn by the men. Thank heavens fifty years on and modern uniforms, both for men and women, have been made much more practical. And of course trousers for policewomen were unheard of in the seventies.

As all police leave had been cancelled there were officers on the scene quickly, with firemen, ambulances and taxis too. We automatically formed a chain, passing victims along to waiting ambulances and taxis. Some could walk but were dazed and bleeding, with some needing to be carried.

I arrived home in the early hours to find my husband frantic with worry, having arrived a few minutes before me. He had been unable to contact me since we had left home earlier in the day, not knowing where I was and when, or even if, I would arrive home. He told me he never wanted me to go out to work again and we both sobbed in each other's arms, as we discussed the dreadful, shocking incident that had happened.

Yet I was back at work the next morning by 9am as I was required at Crown Court on another case.

During the weeks that followed I was involved in sorting property that had been recovered from the scene. We had to list it and return it to next of kin where possible. I particularly remember that handbag and other personal items retrieved from the scenes of carnage. Although difficult, it was a privilege to return these to the families whose lives had been devastated and changed forever.

During the months and even years that followed, it was a difficult time for many Irish people living in Birmingham. My husband's auntie by marriage, who lived in the city, didn't like to go out too much afterwards and when she did, she tried to disguise her accent for fear of reprisals. She felt ashamed about what had happened.

I like to think that times have changed and in 2024 we are now a more open and accepting society.

Sadly that is not always the case.

Forty five years later I was called to give evidence at the Inquest into the deaths that had occurred. I met with several colleagues I hadn't seen for years.

It was a very sad experience but at the same time interesting and exhausting.

I was doing my job, no more, no less that night and it is easy with hindsight to say some things could have been done differently, especially when communications systems were so much more primitive than they are today.

I am fortunate that I come from a large close family and I had married into another large family in Birmingham. Whilst I believe that counselling has a very important part to play in dealing with trauma, having my family around me helped me realise how lucky I was not to have been physically injured myself. With their support I was able to recover, to continue doing the job I loved and I carried on for several more years until we were fortunate to have a family of our own.

It was horrendous on that particular night for many people, as they lost their loved ones. I consider myself to be one of the fortunate ones.

What happened that night will always be in my memory and on each November 21st at 8.20pm I still pay homage to all those that lost their lives and were affected by the events.

JOHN PLIMMER'S STORY

The 21st November 1974 is a date etched permanently in the memory of many people and in particular those citizens of Birmingham, the UK's second largest city. As was the case with the assassination of President John F Kennedy in Houston, Texas, many remember exactly where they were and what they were doing when terrorism brought multiple murders, immense mourning and shame to the city centre.

I can recollect it was a typically dark and damp November night with the sounds of Abba, Queen, Barry White, Showaddywaddy and other favourite entertainment artists of that time bellowing out from the various entertainment venues. Being a Thursday, it was busy with revellers and people about to enjoy a night on the town. Bright lights still reflected out from shop frontages with some of them open late in the run up to Christmas. What would have been missed on that particular night was the noticeable absence of patrolling police officers, who were usually out mingling with the crowds. The reason for that was simple; the city centre had been stripped of its uniformed law enforcement capacity, in favour of added security at Birmingham Airport.

A week prior to the 21st November, James McDade, a member of the Provisional IRA, had blown himself up when planting a terrorist bomb at the Coventry Telephone Exchange. On November 21st arrangements had been made for McDade's body to be flown back home to the Irish Republic from

Birmingham Airport and there were genuine fears that anti-British protests could take place around the airport concourse, resulting in some serious disorder. Hence the requirement for officers to be transferred away from their normal duties some fifteen miles or so away from the city centre.

'Big Brum', the clock supported by the Chamberlain Tower at the Birmingham Council House, had already chimed eight o'clock. The Tavern in the Town and Mulberry Bush public houses, both situated in the city's New Street, were filled to capacity with mostly young people enjoying the warm atmosphere of relaxation and merriment, unaware of the devastating atrocities that were to take place.

Bombs exploded in both establishments that night, causing the deaths of 21 people with around 200 others being left injured, a good number of them with life-changing injuries. The city centre of Birmingham became one of chaos, shock, anger and disorientation, as the few and insufficient emergency service people first on the scene, attempted to rescue survivors.

Much has been written about the incidents of that dreadful night. Some accounts have been recorded accurately, although in a piece-meal fashion. Unfortunately, for whatever macabre reasons, some of the comments made by people claiming to have witnessed the series of events that followed the explosions are not true and misleading.

Two detective officers were present in the city centre on that fateful night and visited the Tavern in the Town, just before the bomb detonated at that location. As a young detective, I was one of them, accompanied by Detective Sergeant Mike Davey.

The evening began when we both strolled along New Street, heading for the Odeon Cinema where we intended to take a statement from an usherette who had witnessed an earlier robbery. We had already arrested and charged a couple of youths before allowing them bail a few days earlier. The manager of the cinema confirmed the person we wanted to see wasn't working on that particular night, so arrangements were made to see her the following evening, leaving us with some time to spare.

I suggested to Mike that I could introduce him to Dick Lawn, the licensee at the nearby Tavern in the Town licensed premises and he agreed. After walking the hundred yards or so along New Street, we finally reached the entrance to the Tavern before heading down the stairway, which led to the main underground bar. The cold damp air outside was quickly forgotten as we entered the warmth of a room almost full to capacity with people involved in conversations, drinking and enjoying a night out.

After making our way through to the bar we were disappointed to be told by one of the barmen that his employer was away, visiting friends.

I remember Mike quipping that we weren't having much luck that evening, before ordering two glasses of lager.

We stood for a short time with our drinks, leaning against a supporting pole near the centre of the room. You certainly could not have swung a cat around in that crowded location and I checked my watch to see if we still had time for another drink. We did, so I offered to buy another round.

Mike declined, explaining that he still had work to finish back at Digbeth Police Station, our place of employment. Little did either of us know at that time, Mike Davey's refusal to have another drink, could well have saved our lives.

It was just approaching 8pm when we stepped back out into New Street and made our way in the general direction of Digbeth, passing the front of the Mulberry Bush public house, which was on our right.

We continued down through the open market in the so-called 'Bull Ring', with its many stalls now empty and standing like shadows in the darkness.

Although I cannot recall the subject of our conversation as we progressed down Digbeth towards the police station, I do remember we were both laughing about something that would have been innocuous and unimportant.

Then about a hundred yards from our destination we were suddenly stopped in our tracks by the too familiar sound of a bomb exploding. Having experienced our fair share of devices being detonated in the city centre, usually targeting the Rotunda, a cylindrical building which overlooked both New Street and the Bull Ring Centre, we both assumed it was yet another repetitive attempt. No matter how many occasions terrorist efforts had been on that same landmark, it still stood proud and defiant.

Following that first explosion I remember looking up to confirm the Rotunda building was still standing in all its glory. In fact, I joked that the IRA wouldn't rest until they'd managed to totally demolish Birmingham's most recent and famous city centre building. Then we heard a second explosion, muffled and distant, but realising instantly it was a second bomb.

As we were so close to Digbeth station, we ran inside to ask if they had any information as to where the explosions had taken place, but what few officers we found were as mystified as we were. Then the radio controller, Billy Wilson, told us he'd received a report that one bomb had gone off inside Yates's Wine Lodge in Corporation Street, near to the junction with New Street and that there were two people trapped on the roof there. He had no means to respond quickly, his usual quota being engaged in the airport operation.

Of course, looking back it had been an error to leave the centre of Birmingham so exposed, although I personally believe that no matter how many officers might have been retained, it would not have prevented the atrocities that took place. However, at least more immediate support would have been available during the recovery attempts at both premises attacked.

We both fled back up the hill towards New Street and somehow got separated. I reached the Wine Lodge where I was met by a very nervous barman, who led me up some flights of stairs to where there was a door accessing the roof.

It's amazing how people react to situations when consumed by fear. When I actually got on to the roof it was dark, but I could make out two figures standing at the far end. It was the licensee and his wife, who having heard the explosions and believing it was their premises being attacked, phoned the police thinking that the safest place to be was up on the roof.

I left Yates's Wine Lodge and returned to New Street, just a few yards away, which appeared quiet with a few people continuing on their individual ways. I was still oblivious to where the bombs had been detonated but still favouring the Rotunda.

All that changed when I found Mike Davey, or rather his voice, coming up from the pavement just outside the entrance to the Tavern in the Town, which was then in total darkness. He was yelling for me to retrace our steps down where we had gone earlier to visit the licensee. At first it was difficult, slowly descending the stairs in total darkness, the air thick with smoke with a strong sickly smell of cordite. Even then, I felt a confused as to where the seats of the explosions were located, but not for long.

By the time I reached the bottom of the stairs my eyes had

adjusted to the darkness. Despite feeling disoriented, I managed to seek out Mike who was crouching over something on the floor just a few feet away.

There was nothing visible that resembled the Tavern's appearance when we had gone there just a short time beforehand. Now all I could see was a dust cloud and bodies lying all over the floor, some groaning, and others, motionless and silent. It was all so surreal but for whatever reason the only priority was to get as many of the injured out of there and as quickly as possible. A fear of another device exploding didn't enter my mind and neither did the thought of how many fatalities there were. The only priority was the need to get what casualties were alive out of there as quickly as possible.

Mike called out that we needed to get them up the stairs and onto the street. I looked down at the face of a young girl lying on the floor, staring up at me. We needed urgent help but there was no other option but to do all we could until assistance arrived, God knows where from though.

Kneeling down beside the casualty, I tried to reassure her that she would be alright but we had to get back to the safety of the street above our heads. I then carefully lifted her from the carpet and held her in my arms. It was then I felt as if I had been hit by a thunderbolt. The girl flopped forward in my arms, and I could see the back of her head had been removed by the blast. I could feel my legs start to tremble as I carefully placed her body back down on the floor. She had gone and reality kicked in to remind me that there were others who were still breathing. It was those who we had to search for through the thick smoke and attend to against a background of people groaning and talking incoherently.

By that time, Mike had disappeared up the stairs carrying a casualty and I quickly began to replicate his rescue work. We were joined by firemen and local taxi drivers, who helped us to carry the injured up the stairs into the street, where we made them as comfortable as possible on the damp pavements. Neither of us had time to pause, chasing back down the stairs, returning to street level with another victim and continuing without interruption or time to think about what had taken place. At one stage I did stop to look at a line of casualties, all with serious injuries, lying on the floor with their backs resting against shop frontages. There were observers who attempted to provide what first aid and reassurance they could, but it was obvious that many of the victims had to be hospitalised fast. A line of taxi drivers were quickly transporting the injured to the local hospitals, returning very quickly to pick up more of those poor and unfortunate people.

And yet, there was no emotion being displayed, no tears, no outrage at what had happened, just a determination to empty that underground public house of every living human being. No time to think or contemplate or even step back to consider what we were doing, only a recognition of the speed required to carry individually injured people up those damned stairs and away from that place of carnage.

One young lady was sitting in the smoke-filled darkness at a point furthest away from the exit, staring out from a pale and expressionless face. At first I thought she had suffered in the same way as the first girl I had earlier lifted from the floor, but decided to ask how she was.

"It's my leg," she gasped, thankfully confirming that she was alive.

The injury she had sustained was horrendous. What looked like the wooden leg of a bar stool had penetrated through her lower leg and thigh, pinning both parts of her limb. With the help of a fire fighter, we both managed to cradle the victim in our arms and carefully carry her up the stairs and to the safety of the street pavement. She was in agonising pain and we tried to be as gentle as possible, lowering her to the pavement to sit with the other victims leaning against a shop frontage. Although in shock, her discomfort eased a little as the tears continued to cascade down each side of her face. Before returning to the underground bar, we pleaded with one of the taxi drivers to take her to hospital as a priority, which he did.

More mostly young men and women, some with horrific life-threatening injuries and all suffering severely from shock, were extracted from the Tavern in the Town. When we were satisfied that no one had been left inside who was still alive, we stood in the night air catching our breath. But even then, there was still work to be done, after being told that another bomb had exploded inside the Mulberry Bush, just a few hundred yards away.

Even during the time we were still engaged at the Tavern in the Town, a few groups of individuals gathered at the far end of New Street. They were shouting and screaming abuse aimed towards the Irish population, sparking a great deal of anger, hatred and bitterness that was to eventually increase in intensity across the city.

By that time, more police officers began to appear at the two crime scenes, relieving those members of the public who had so gallantly helped us to save those who survived, those whose lives would never be the same again.

Whilst making our way along New Street towards the Mulberry Bush, the reality of what had taken place struck home with a vengeance, resulting in both myself and Mike Davey feeling nauseous. We stepped down an alleyway alongside the Odeon Cinema and could not avoid being physically sick. However, having phoned home to assure our own families that we were safe and unharmed, we both remained on duty until well into the following morning. After I returned to my home to my wife and three year old son to snatch a few hours' sleep, I recall suddenly trembling and could not stop weeping as if the shock of what I had witnessed during those previous few hours had suddenly hit home.

The next day, Mike and I sat down together and just talked through what had happened to us. It was our own way of dealing with it, two colleagues and friends finding ourselves in the midst of a horrific event while out doing our job.

After returning to work, there was not much we could do at either of the scenes of carnage, leaving the necessary tasks to the Fire Service and forensic teams. For a while I personally found it difficult to concentrate on my own daily work commitments, knowing it would take some time before I could fully return to my duties prior to the atrocities.

Those of us who had the misfortune of being there didn't speak of the circumstances for many years to come. For us, there was no meeting of the inevitable dignitaries who later attended both scenes; no attending any kind of money raising events that also took place or any kind of congratulatory recognition for those who assisted in the rescuing. The events themselves had been so disturbing none of us had any desire to prolong the traumatic memories of what happened on 21 November 1974 and we didn't discuss the circumstances with even our own senior officers.

As far as the city of Birmingham was concerned, the atmosphere within its boundaries became almost unbearable, especially for those of Irish origin. My own mother-in-law who was born in County Monaghan and who was the most gentile lady you could ever wish to meet, was subjected to various levels of abuse during those few days that followed. Incidents involving attacks on Irish people were reported frequently and myself and many of my colleagues could only feel sympathy for those who, through no fault of their own, became the victims of mindless and unjust upheaval.

From a personal point of view, did I feel any anger towards those responsible? Yes without doubt. Would I have liked to see them hang for their atrocities? No, only to see justice obtained for the victims. Did I suffer from any post trauma syndrome as a result of the activities on that fateful night? I would say no, and yet, many years after I had retired from the police, when giving evidence to the Coroner's Inquest in 2019, I actually reached a point when I found it difficult to give my evidence and felt for the first time in my life, emotionally disturbed when describing the events at the Tavern in the Town.

Finally, my personal tribute to the late Mike Davey:

Before the dreadful events on 21st November 1974, both myself and Mike Davey were close friends and colleagues. Our shared experiences that night undoubtedly created an even closer bond between us lasting throughout the remainder of Mike's lifetime. Sadly, his recent passing has been met with widespread sorrow and regret by many who knew him, not least than by myself. The courage and inspiration he often displayed to me personally and the care and compassion he projected on that particular night will always stay with me. My deepest condolences go out to his four sons and their families.

MAURICE MALONE'S STORY
(As told to Enda Mullen)

Maurice Malone's story is one of personal resilience and triumph over adversity, creating something good out of the trauma his own family experienced in the wake of the Birmingham bombings.

As the now Chief Executive of Birmingham Irish Association (BIA), Maurice has played an important role in remembering and commemorating the victims of the Birmingham pub bombings.

It began back In 2015 when BIA held a witness seminar at the University of Birmingham to gather and record memories of the terrible events of that fateful night in November 1974 and their historical importance.

The event saw a diverse panel of speakers, including survivors, people from the families who lost their lives, members of the emergency services who attended the scenes of the bombings and representatives of Birmingham's Irish communities.

The aim was to record stories but also to try to understand how the pub bombings impacted on people, communities, and the city itself.

One of the key things that emerged from the seminar was a desire to have a fitting memorial, with a strong feeling that an existing one by St Philip's Cathedral was not enough. What also emerged during the seminar was the damage done to

Birmingham's Irish community, both in the immediate aftermath but also as an enduring legacy.

This prompted Maurice to set up the Misneach Memorial Committee, which brought together a range of Irish organisations, the University of Birmingham, Birmingham City Council and victims' families - with the aim of lobbying for and organising a prominent memorial in the heart of the city.

The culmination of all this was a striking memorial installed at the concourse of Birmingham New Street Station in November 2018.

The memorial comprises three large metal trees with the names of the victims punched into their leaves, marking the city with the identities of those who never came home that night.

Funded by Network Rail and the Irish government it has won widespread praise and also serves as the location for a memorial service held on the anniversary of the pub bombings each year.

Although Maurice and his family were not physical victims of the pub bombings, the events of November 21st 1974 had a devastating impact on his family, leading to the break-up of the family unit and Maurice not seeing his father for 15 years.

Maurice was just eight years old at the time of the pub bombings and up until then had been enjoying an idyllic childhood in his close and loving family at the heart of a tight-knit community in Chelmsley Wood, north Solihull.

He said: "We were a typical immigrant family, mum and dad moved over from Dublin to work over here. They ended up in a place called Chelmsley Wood, a staunch Irish Catholic community.

"Mum and dad settled there and I came along in 1967".

Maurice's father worked at the Bakelite factory in Tyseley and his mum ran the household.

"Our school was 100 per cent white Irish Catholic," said Maurice. "A tight-knit community that was very supportive of each other."

Although Maurice was just eight his recollections of the event are still crystal clear.

He said: "I was in bed, it was a Thursday night, a school day the next day. I could hear shouting and voices and stuff. It must have broke on the news what had happened. Mum and dad were having some sort of discussion or argument, I didn't think any more as an eight-year-old.

"I remember the next morning, breakfast, it was strange - dad wasn't talking. He went off to work."

Maurice was greeted by the shocking sight of a large police presence at his school, which was just a short walk away, that morning.

"I remember going there and there were police officers at the gate of the school," he said. "They were inside the playground. I thought they had come to say hello to the children - back then you had bobbies on the beat. I sort of thought they were there for reassurance. They were here for a different reason, there were quite a few, a dozen.

The start of the school day saw the children given an explanation of the tragic events of the previous evening in Birmingham city centre.

Maurice said: "We went into our classes - we were taught by nuns - they started explaining to us what had happened and said we weren't allowed to go out to play. It was not a lockdown as such but we weren't allowed to play outside.

"School finished early and my mum was at the gate for me, she had never done that before. I was trying to piece together what had happened the night before and work out why our school life had changed, why she was at the gate. I said bombs had gone off last night, she said we will talk about it at home."

Maurice was not prepared for the sight that greeted him at home - his father had returned from work when ordinarily he would still be there.

"Dad was at home, he had got cuts and bruises," he said. "Mum started crying. For an eight-year-old this was all getting to me. Dad didn't speak, which was really out of character for him."

Maurice's mother tried to expand on what he had been told at school, saying that bombs had gone off and they thought people from Ireland had done it.

That day Maurice started to get a sense of the effect of the bombings on the Irish community.

"During the afternoon I remember getting a lot of visitors to the house," he said. "It was a bit like a wake, with all the sandwiches out. Adults were talking about what had happened and how things had changed for them."

The impact of the bombings on Maurice's family began to be revealed the following morning.

"Dad normally did weekend shifts but he was still in the house," said Maurice. "He opened up, he had gone into work on the Friday morning. Quite a lot of Irish lads worked there, they were attacked by British workers at the factory.

"These were guys who were best mates 24 hours before. He would go out with those people and play dominoes and darts. In effect they were sacked - told to go home. He said to me people had come over from Ireland and put bombs in the city centre and we had to stay close and look after each other. That was the end of his job and he never went back to the Bakelite."

Maurice said that "life sort of stood still". Friends, family, cousins were coming around talking about it and although he was still going to school he said the family didn't really go out anywhere.

Other than school he might go to the park with his mother, when she would "try to not talk", as she feared people hearing her Irish accent.

For Maurice's family life would never be the same again.

"Dad didn't go out other than to the corner shop to get his fags," said Maurice. "Things for my family went downhill from there - life in school was difficult and life in the community was difficult. Dad started to go very quickly downhill.

"He liked a drink but he started drinking quite heavily, to the point where he was more drunk than sober most of the day.

"There were rows between him and my mum and he got hands on with her when he had had a drink.

"It was like life stood still for us in this capsule in our own house and we were afraid to go out into the real world. Mum and dad's relationship deteriorated."

Maurice recalls the police at the house after his father had "taken it out" on his mother and even the parish priest visiting to try and help the family.

"I remember having a conversation with my dad, I put my arms around him and he cried," said Maurice.

"I knew the path he was on, he was full of guilt about letting me down, letting his family down."

Some of the lowest points were when his father was arrested and spent nights in the cells but Maurice said he would just come out and drink again and the cycle continued.

Reflecting on the bombings and the consequences for his family, Maurice said: "21 people died that night, a lot of people were hurt and had life-changing injuries.

"When I look back now it sounds strange but my dad died that night. The life he had built for us, his life, his social network all crumbled on that evening.

"He didn't have the resilience to fight back and get past it but there were lots of people who were literally prisoners in their own homes.

"That went on for weeks. Even though I was only eight I had a feeling that mum and dad's marriage was done. Mum had had enough both mentally and physically, his drinking was getting extreme - a couple of bottles of whiskey a day.

"He was rotting away, which was sad to see. He was a big hulk of a man and turned into an alcoholic and one who couldn't see a way out.

"It went on for months. Dad moved out of the house, back to Whitehall in Dublin. Mum couldn't cope with him anymore.

"He was always my hero, I looked up to him. To lose the role model out of your life. I knew he was never coming back."

"I knew that was the end of our family, which was devastating for a young kid like me."

It was the start of a long period of separation from his father for Maurice and when he did see him again, the man he had so looked up to was a shell of his former self.

"I didn't see him for 15 years," said Maurice. "He didn't want to come back to Birmingham. I remember going to see him, he was in a bedsit in Ballymun. It was an awful hovel of a place with a one ring cooker, filthy dirty.

"I remember walking in thinking oh my god, my hero who I adored has become this shell of a man. I spent a week with him and couldn't wait to get home. He wasn't the man I had known.

"Next time I saw him he was dead. He had a heart attack when he was on holiday in Bulgaria. He was in a casket they had transported him in, in Whitehall, Dublin."

However Maurice does remember life getting back to some sort of normality after his father had left. He said his mother "ploughed on" and got a job at the Cadbury factory in Bournville.

"By then things had relented," said Maurice. "You could get back out, normal things started to come back into our lives - playing out with friends, day trips, holidays. Life got back to normal to some extent but without my dad.

"My personal loss was losing my family unit and my dad. If that (the bombings) hadn't have happened my dad would still be here, there would have been no reason to go down the route he did. All because he was Irish and had an Irish accent."

BREDA POWER'S STORY

As a 9 year old child in 1975, Breda Power remembers vividly visiting her father at Wormwood Scrubs prison in London.

Before then she was led to believe that her dad was in hospital.

'Of course once I saw the prison notice I knew where we were going but it was as if mum was trying to convince us that dad was in hospital. Hammersmith Hospital was next door and mum walked us past it on the way into the prison.'

Breda is the daughter of William Power, one of the six men who were given 21 life sentences in 1975 after a lengthy court case held at Lancaster Castle. Known as the Birmingham Six, they stood accused of planting the bombs in the two packed out Birmingham pubs on November 21st 1974. Breda's father and the other men – Hugh Callaghan, Patrick Hill, Richard McIlkenny, Gerard Hunter and John Walker - spent 16 and a half years in prison until their release on their third appeal in 1991.

Breda doesn't recall much about her early childhood living in Birmingham in the years before the bombings. At the time her mum Nora was in her late 20s with four children and was a stay-at-home parent. She had come over to Birmingham from Cork to find work and escape poverty. It was here that she met Breda's dad known as 'Billy' Power who was from a big family in north Belfast and was just 21 when they got married. The couple settled in the Aston area of the city and Breda and her sister were born within 10 months of each other. Two other siblings followed quickly.

In 1974 the family had moved to Erdington and Breda vividly remembers the aftermath of the bombings.

'The tragic event happened on the Thursday night but my sharpest memory is of the Sunday night following it,' she says, recalling that she and her siblings were allowed to stay up later because they were waiting for her dad to come home.

'We were all sat in our night clothes on the couch watching telly. Then there was a news flash with the images of the six men including my dad and it said they had caught the Birmingham bombers.'

'As children we didn't know exactly what had happened but we knew it was something bad and that people had been killed. So my immediate reaction was that my dad was one of the dead.'

Breda recalls her mum dropping a tray of biscuits she was carrying and running out of the house.

'I then remember us going into the next door neighbour's house and me and my sister stayed there while the younger two went to another neighbour a couple of doors away. These neighbours were local Birmingham people and they were really good to my mum.'

'I know some of the other families were chased away from their homes but our neighbours were amazing that night while mum went off to the police station to find dad.'

The following day Breda and her sister were put on a plane to Cork on their own, their fare paid for by their mum's brother. Within a week they were placed in a local Catholic school and weren't allowed to mix outside the classroom with the other children there.

'At break times and lunch times we were segregated and taken into a little room. The nuns who taught us were kind, giving us a snack and milk. I suppose you have to remember that everybody must have thought my dad and the five others had done the bombings. I guess there was a feeling around at that point that they might have done it.'

Breda adds that it was a horrendous time because as children nobody talked to them about what had happened. She remembers not really knowing if her dad was alive or dead.

When Breda and her sister returned to Birmingham, she was told by her mum that her dad was in hospital and believed he was recovering from injuries.

During the trial of the six at Lancaster Castle in the summer of 1975, Breda and her siblings went to stay with her dad's family in Belfast. Away from what was happening in Birmingham, they were looked after by their uncle Eddie, one of her dad's brothers who Breda says was amazing, giving up a big part of his life to take care of them.

After the six men were found guilty of planting the bombs and sentenced, there was a brief but unhappy return to Birmingham.

Breda's dad was then moved to Wormwood Scrubs prison in London which was next to Hammersmith Hospital. The family moved down to London to be near to him.

'On the way to visit dad for the first time mum walked us past the hospital with its signage. Of course I knew by then that we were going into the prison but it was as if she was trying to convince us that dad was in hospital.'

'We went into the prison waiting area and when they called us they said we were there "to visit the bombers". I just felt sick and when we got to see dad he was so happy because he hadn't seen us for months.'

Still only aged 10, Breda became a carer to her three younger siblings while her mum found work.

'My mum had early morning jobs, after school jobs working in factories and doing manual work. Often I would get everyone up and ready for school, get breakfast, walk the younger two to primary school before me and my sister would head to junior school about half a mile away. When we got home I would make me and my siblings a light meal – something that didn't take much cooking like beans or spaghetti on toast.

'My mum used to go out with some of my dad's family and all of them were still young. My mum used to socialise with them rather than just staying in the house crying that my dad was in jail. So I found myself baby-sitting and getting the kids to bed.'

Breda says alcohol was an issue and although the cupboards were full and the children were well dressed, emotionally her mum was dealing with her own issues.

As she became more settled at secondary school, Breda started to do well academically considering the disruption to her earlier education. It wasn't until she was around 15 that she began to take an interest in her dad's case, going through the case file, finding anomalies in the evidence and writing to the Queen and the then Prime Minister Margaret Thatcher to reopen the case.

Over the next few years Breda focused on the campaign to free the six, working with campaigners Paul May, Chris Mullin and lawyers Gareth Pierce and Michael Mansfield. In 1991 the Birmingham Six were freed after 16 and a half years in prison and two failed appeals.

'On the day I just remember telling myself to be in the moment, otherwise I wouldn't remember all the details. So I just absorbed every bit,'

Years of visiting her father in prison and campaigning was the start of her interest in the prison system and ultimately led to the job that she is doing today. Breda now works as a senior case manager with the Irish Council for Prisoners Overseas (ICPO) a project of the Irish Chaplaincy, a social action charity providing services and support to excluded, vulnerable and isolated Irish people in England and Wales.

'In the beginning our family was a service user of the Irish Chaplaincy and the Irish Council for Prisoners Overseas' says Breda, adding that they were 'an enormous support at a time early on when nobody wanted to know us.'

What started as an administrative job to cover sick leave in 2005 became a full time job which involved training as case worker. In her working role Breda has access to nearly all the London prisons including Wormwood Scrubs where she used to visit her dad, Wandsworth and Brixton. Her work involves dealing with probation officers, prison staff and other professionals, not just with the prisoners themselves but also their families.

In the course of her training she has undergone trauma counselling which has helped her to process her own difficult childhood experiences in the wake of her father's high profile conviction and ultimate release.

'As a child it was all too much to take in. You don't process it either but that's a coping mechanism and it is amazing how resilient kids are. It was only when I started to go through adolescence when the penny dropped and I started to realise what I had been through.'

Breda says that she sees herself as a resource for other

professional workers involved with prisoners and their families

Although conditions for children visiting prison have improved over the years, recent economic pressures mean many families cannot afford to visit regularly. Her work involves helping prisoners financially which is important to their rehabilitation.

Breda welcomes initiatives like 'Story Book Dads' enabling a number of prisoners to record stories for their children, so that they can hear their voices outside of a prison setting. She recalls hearing her dad's voice on the phone for the first time during the 1991 appeal and how he sounded different from when she spoke to him in prison.

After almost 20 years of working in prisons, it is the use of her own lived experience that gives her the most satisfaction and she refers to a case of a 45 year old man who had been in and out of prison for almost 25 years. After helping him to access educational courses inside prison, she helped him get accommodation when he was released and to get his first ever passport. He was delighted telling her 'this as good as it gets.'

Reflecting on her childhood experiences Breda comments:

'I know in my own family there is inter-generational trauma as a result of what happened – mental health issues, addictions. It's a ripple and domino effect, too much of drowning the sorrows, feelings of helplessness and hopelessness. It affected all of us.'

Despite this, her message to her eight year old self is one of resilience and hope.

'You won't always be a victim; you won't always feel shame; you will be vindicated; you will go on to help others as you have been helped; never stop believing; forgive easily; miracles happen.'

PAUL AM PALMER'S STORY

(SOMEONE ELSE: LOSING MY VOICE)

When I first came to England as a 10 year-old child in 1971 it was to escape the so-called 'Troubles' in Northern Ireland and a near brush with death. Just three years after being taken to what I thought was a place of safety, the Birmingham bombings made my life more difficult and I went back to that frightened child who had left Belfast.

When British soldiers first came to Belfast, they made me, my brother and three sisters laugh. Like most families in the neighbourhood, we made them tea and, being a child at the time the reasons for them being there didn't seem to matter. We still went to school; we still played football after dinner until bedtime; and we still had that one game of rounders in the summer when the entire estate converged on our street to join in.

Then something changed, although as children we had no idea why. We no longer made tea for the squaddies and they no longer made us laugh. We had bomb scares at school, children flooding out through the gates into the arms of tearful mothers and aunties and grannies. We all heard the shots that killed an unarmed man near the shops at the top of the road and we weren't allowed to go near there until the blood stains began to disappear from sight.

Other events soon came into play. My dad was already finding it hard to find work, and then the shooting came too close to home. In summer's long school holiday, my cousins, my brother and me were playing in a scrapped car propped up on bricks in scrubland near the motorway, on our own road to nowhere. Suddenly we heard the crack of a rifle being fired, and shortly after that another crack followed as the bullet whistled past my face. We turned and saw an army jeep on the motorway, then we ran, screaming and stumbling back to our homes. The entire street seemed to flood with people, all flowing towards our house, seeping through the front and back doors. Neighbours gathered in the back garden wondering what had happened as we trembled and wept in the arms of our mothers. We were told later that a sniper was using us as cover while waiting to shoot at the next army patrol to drive by. The scrubland was out of bounds after that, so we had to make do with endless games of football or Cowboys and Indians.

For dad, this shooting was the final straw and he left Belfast to go and look for work, landing in Wales and sending postcards back to each of us (two sons and three daughters) as we had no phone in our house. He loved Llanelli and the Welsh were more than welcoming and helpful. Although he had work, he couldn't find a suitable house, so ended up in Yorkshire, where a job and then a house soon followed.

When the time finally came for us to leave Belfast, we spent the week before the journey sorting out our toys for packing - we used the dog kennel my dad had made (she refused to sleep in it!). On the day we left I don't recall being upset - this was all to be a big adventure and I remember we all had a comic to read on the journey, not realising how long that would be.

The overnight ferry to Heysham in Lancashire took place not

long after Guy Fawkes' night, but there were no fireworks allowed in Ireland at that time. It was a horrible journey across the sea - the boat seemed full of drunken football fans being sick everywhere. We were glad to get off the boat and onto the trains that took us to our home in Yorkshire, and I still shudder slightly when I find myself in Leeds railway station because the lifts didn't work and we had to climb the stairs to cross to the platform with all our bags and the dog! The local parish priest was amazing - he had organised a van to pick us up and take us from the railway station to our house. The van seemed to stop just minutes after we had set off and we spilled out of the back of it into a house with yellowed newspaper on the windows before wandering around our new home, drinking tea.

I started junior school the week after we arrived, but was misplaced by the headteacher and landed in the final year of junior school, a year younger than my peers. I was embarrassed before I opened my mouth to speak because I didn't understand some of their words ("laking football" meant "playing football"), so I stood like an idiot with a reddening face and when I did speak, people laughed at my accent. Thankfully, I was a decent footballer and found some relief while any match was in progress.

The phrase "He's Irish!" began the snakes and ladders of my schooldays, dogged by the instant prejudice that followed. Apparently, I was thick, stupid and much more. But then came the maths lesson, where I was the only child in class who knew their times-tables backwards and demonstrating an ability for mathematical concepts like long division. This academic awareness just made me stand out a little more than I'd have anticipated. I prepared myself for the big school, but the headteacher suddenly realised that I had been put in the wrong class, so I had to sit the same curriculum for a second time, where I was again the butt of endless jokes from a small set of new hecklers.

Terrible acts of violence and murder in Northern Ireland were always on the TV news and in the papers, with each major event bringing more verbal abuse and mickey-taking. Then in 1974, the dreadful Birmingham pub bombings made things a lot worse, with pupils pointing the finger and blaming me or my relatives for the atrocities, tarring all Irish people with the same ignorant brush. We were seen by some as the enemy within, not to be trusted and treated with suspicion.

Thankfully, I was never physically attacked, but I soon realised that whatever vestiges of Belfast accent I had by then just needed to disappear in a desperate attempt to escape the abuse and fit in. This seems foolish now, given that everyone was aware that I was Irish and never let me forget it, but I suppose I thought that kids wouldn't mimic my accent if I didn't have one.

In the end it didn't make any difference. Even though I played football and socialised with classmates, it was at times a relentless round of daily verbal bullying. Then someone decided that burying my satchel of books in the long jump sand was the very least I deserved. Looking back, I guess that my brother might have had a worse time than me, with his speech impediment probably adding to his woes. As for my sisters, they seemed less affected, just getting on with things as best they could and even competing in Irish dancing. Throughout the years that followed, some maturity crept in but the childish jibes kept coming. I developed a keen wit and strong sense of humour along with a thicker skin, throwing banter back in the direction from whence it came.

The notion of cultural identity would have been lost on me back then, when I simply considered myself Irish and from Belfast. We always had an Irish fry at Christmas and, although shamrock rarely travelled well, we celebrated St Patrick's Day by wearing something green. Even today I can barely get through 'Hail Glorious St Patrick' without getting tearful, the memory of isolation playing a part in that. At home dad still made potato bread, and mum soda bread and a dish we called champ (mash potato mixed with spring onions) or Irish stew. All of these were reminders of where we had come from, but our accents were changed forever.

I'm not sure how much the bombings affected my parents socially or (in my dad's case) at work. The miners' strike of the early 70s encouraged dad to leave the pit and become a labourer on building sites, but he soon went back to the mines because the money simply wasn't sufficient with my youngest sister being born - there were now six children to feed and clothe, adding a financial strain to match that for space.

Then dad found an amazing terraced house just up the road - we were all going to have our own room and joined in the cleaning from the top in the attic all the way to the ground floor. Just before exchanging contracts the conveyancer said he had found out that there was a planning application to demolish the house. I got the impression that dad didn't believe him and that it might just have been a made-up excuse not to sell to an Irish family. Rather irritatingly, the house is still there and the memory grieves me when I drive past it.

Thanks to some hard work in trying circumstances, I escaped to study at a polytechnic in Coventry, where life was so much easier because the students were more grown up, with only the odd jibe about my background and I could still do a mean Frank Carson impersonation if I had to!

I could spot any new Northern Irish students in the town centre because they were the only ones putting their hands up to be searched as they entered Woolworths, BHS and other stores because that's how things were 'back home'. Thankfully, it didn't take too long before this habit ceased. Dad never lost his accent and by the time I was in the Midlands, he was working as a railway signalman. Dad was very proud of my achievements, much to the annoyance of his colleagues who seemed very anti-Irish, eventually hounding him out of the job he enjoyed so much.

So where do all these events leave me? This is a greatly edited version of my life, describing how things were at the time - I bear no malice or bad feeling towards any of my tormentors. "Kids can be terrible" is something I've heard many times - a euphemism for bullying - and I can sadly say that I've witnessed this too many times to count, even from those I thought were my friends. When some Ugandan Asians, as they were referred to, arrived in our area I made a real effort to befriend one of the children who was my age. Eddy's experience was different from mine, but he still found himself in a strange land with a strange accent and I could readily relate to that. We became good friends at the time, though lost touch when I moved south to further my studies.

Since my days at the polytechnic, I've been proud to be Irish and share my heritage, even though I now feel a little detached from the language and culture. If you hear me speak today you would never know that I spent the first 10 years of my life in Belfast.

Memories of growing up in Northern Ireland, fishing in season with dad, and climbing and camping in the mountains of Mourne - these provide rich sources of inspiration for my poetry, another inherited trait from dad. After a radio interview, I fell into a conversation about my lack of a Belfast accent, which provided the key to expressing something that I had been trying to unlock for many years: losing the voice of my youth.

The poem below tells this story, but losing my accent is unimportant when compared to the devastating impact that the bombings had. I dedicate *Someone Else: (School Boy in 1974)* to the memory of those who lost their lives and loved ones and livelihoods at the hands of much worse bullies than those I encountered at school.

Someone Else (School Boy in 1974)

The boy spoke strangely,
while others poked fun at
his clamouring to be heard,
and all the while he wished
that he was someone else.

In other places,
down The Bush and The Tavern,
adults sat and stood and smiled
and supped and smoked
and swayed or shuffled
as the music filtered through the noise;

they filled every space with
life and laughter,
women giggled like girls or
whispered like witches,
glanced at the men
talking football
or ogling the scene
of lipstick and hair-dos
skirts and tops,
tights and boots,

drinking the atmosphere on tap,
drunk on the endless joy of it all.

Elsewhere in darkened rooms,
low voices mingled
with a poisonous fug,
pondering the fuse already lit,
plotting mayhem and more,
wires and solder and gelignite
bringing instant nothingness
in a split second explosion
of cowardly stupidity,

leaving craters in hearts and buildings,
changing the world forever:
a boy lost his accent,
while in those other places,
lives and loves were lost,
murdered by someone else.

BRENDAN FARRELL'S STORY

Born in Dublin and raised in Cavan, Brendan Farrell emigrated to England in 1952 and joined The Irish Post when it was founded in 1970.

Based in Birmingham, he documented the lives of the Irish community in the Midlands and further afield for more than five decades.

Over the years, Brendan was one of The Irish Post's most loyal and dedicated contributors.

As well as his photographic skills, in those early days he played a key part in the logistics of getting the paper onto the shelves.

At the time it was not uncommon to see him loading papers into the van to get them to shops, churches and Irish Centres across the Midlands.

When I was setting up the BBC documentary programme to mark the 30th anniversary of the bombings in 2004, Brendan was generous in sharing his extensive contacts and we met up on several occasions. He had a wicked sense of humour and any meeting with him was always a joy. Although I suggested that he would be a great interviewee for the programme he modestly declined at first. Then one day during the filming he popped into the production office to take some photos of myself and our film crew for The Irish Post to accompany a piece about the making of the documentary. After he had taken the photographs alongside the nearby canal, we went back to the office and I broached Brendan again about doing an interview. How about we just did a quick chat here and now, especially as the camera and sound operators were already there with their film equipment?

I remember him rolling his eyes before saying something like 'oh go on then' but adding that he hadn't got long. It was a quick but powerful interview and I am so glad we did it.

Brendan died in 2022 but his legacy lives on in the city. With thanks to The Irish Post newspaper, here is a piece first written by Brendan for the 30th anniversary of the bombings reporting on how the Irish community stepped out of the shadow of that dark day to become an integral part of Birmingham's thriving multi-cultural identity.

Maggie Fogarty.

Excerpts from a 2004 archive Irish Post article written by Brendan Farrell and republished here to mark the 50th anniversary of the Birmingham pub bombings

"It will forever go down as one of the darkest days in Birmingham's history.

The evening of November 21st 1974 saw 21 people killed and 182 injured as two IRA bombs exploded within minutes of each other at the Tavern In The Town and Mulberry Bush pubs in the centre of the city.

Those who survived the attacks later described a scene of carnage inside what was left of the two pubs. Debris buried dozens, searing hot timber beams ripped through.

Ireland's bloody war witnessed as something remote until then had arrived in Britain's second city. But while the IRA may have wanted to strike at the heart of Britain it was the Irish community which suffered hardest.

At least 10 per cent of those killed and injured were either Irish or of Irish descent. The last two victims to be identified were brothers Desmond and Eugene Reilly - whose parents hailed from Ireland. And the aftermath of that horrific event created a backlash against the city's Irish community which took decades to heal.

The Irish who had flocked to Birmingham in the 1940s, 50s and 60s in their thousands and built a thriving community suddenly found themselves ostracised by friends and workmates.

Irish-owned buildings were vandalised and prominent members of the Irish community bombarded with death threats. That year the St Patrick's Day annual parade was halted and it seemed the backlash would go on forever.

But nine years later the rebuilding started led by the late Fr. Joe Taffe - Director of the Birmingham Irish Welfare and Information Centre. He restarted the St Patrick's Parade and decreed it was time for the Irish community to come out of the shadows.

Building on that came the formation of the Birmingham Irish Community Forum - providing a link and the first ever official voice for the Irish community in the city.

From the dark days of 1974 an amazing transformation was under way. And its impact has been astonishing and a testament to the strength of the Irish spirit in the city. For nowadays it's not just the Irish community who are proud of what is deemed to be the third largest St. Patrick's Parade in the world. City leaders boast of the event as one of Birmingham's top annual attractions with attendances reaching 130,000.

The new face of Birmingham - a reshaped Bull Ring, the prestigious NEC and Centenary Square - boast stonework fashioned by Mayoman Basil Burke and his Burke Masonry firm. And just as in 1974 every hospital in the city has vital equipment in place paid for by the Irish community's fundraising efforts.

Overseas visitors drop in to the many Irish pubs in the city - especially in the Digbeth area where a six-year project has just begun to build a new Irish Quarter.

But if you want a prime example of how good it is to be Irish in Birmingham these days then look no further than the hugely successful GAA in Schools project - established six years ago by Bishop Challoner School and The Irish Post.

The dark memories of that fateful night in November 1974 will never be forgotten - but today the Irish community stands proudly at the centre of a new Birmingham."

ALFRED WHITE'S STORY

In 1974 I was working a senior registrar in psychiatry at the Birmingham Queen Elizabeth Hospital, in the city where I grew up and went to school.

After completing my medical training in London at Guy's Hospital and then moving to King's College Hospital in 1967, I became interested in psychiatry. While the other parts of medical training involved learning the facts, in psychiatry I had to think more about concepts and ideas. I didn't like living in London back then but met my wife there and we are still together over 50 years later.

I realised that I was more likely to progress in psychiatry if I got a job in Birmingham and approached Professor Sir William Trethowan there who had a good reputation. This was in 1971 and I applied for a surgical houseman post at Birmingham's Queen Elizabeth before moving on to a senior house office post in psychiatry.

A year later I became a registrar there to Dr Andrew Sims who I realised was really talented and he encouraged me to get involved in psychiatric research. Andrew later became a senior lecturer in psychiatry at the University of Birmingham before becoming a professor and president of the Royal College of Psychiatry.

It was Andrew who first suggested that I pursue research at the Birmingham Accident Hospital. At that time it had a world famous burns unit and I started investigating the physical and mental impact of patients with burn injuries compared to those who had suffered other injuries. This research gave me an interest in the relationship between physical injuries and mental illness.

My early research showed that following a severe accident involving burns or other injuries, up to two thirds of individuals were suffering from psychological problems a year afterwards. I wanted to determine how much it was the physical injuries themselves that led to psychological problems compared to the trauma of the incident that caused them.

On the night of the 1974 Birmingham bombings I wasn't at work but recall the huge impact on the city, with 21 people dead and over 100 more injured some of them seriously. Others escaped physically unscathed but were still affected mentally. Surprisingly only one patient was referred to me, an Irish woman who was at the other end of New Street when the bombs went off. She was left traumatised and was referred to me for psychiatric assessment.

Then about two years after the bombings I became involved in a research project with Dr Andrew Sims looking at the impact of the explosions on some of the survivors with less serious injuries. With the pub bombings the majority didn't have significant physical injuries – a good number had perforated ear drums and other non-life-threatening injuries - with 116 being sent home after hospital registration and treatment. Our research was focused on the social and symptomatic effects on a number of these lesser physically injured survivors and a small sub-sample of 20 people affected were visited at home. The mean age of the people interviewed was 21-25 years, with 12 males and 8 females and all were approached approximately two years after the explosions.

(Original study reference below). **

The records of these survivors before and after the bomb explosions were compared to another group of matched hospital outpatient casualties of a similar age, sex and level of injuries. These comparison outpatients had attended the accident hospital casualty department on a Thursday night in the three weeks leading up to the bombings and we called this group the 'attenders'. Like the bombings survivor study group, all had been allowed to return home straight after treatment.

At the time of our follow-up research, 11 of the pub bombing survivors were single, 3 were married and 6 were separated or divorced. Five of this last group put their estrangement at least partly down to the impact of the bombings.

Whilst 15 said they were in good general physical health, 5 described themselves as in poor or very poor health. 70% of the survivors group reported suffering from neurotic or emotionally distressing symptoms to a conspicuous extent over the intervening two years, with several describing phobic symptoms.

Eight of the survivor group required psychotropic medication after the explosions, with some becoming emotionally dependent on their medication.

Nearly half of the survivor study sample said they had problems with employment putting this down to the long-term nervous effects of the bombings, with two claiming to be unemployed due to severe anxiety since the explosions. Three people had changed their job for something less demanding due to 'nerves' with another four reporting that their work had suffered due to their mental state.

Half of the survivor group reported an increase in cigarette smoking since the explosions. While a few had reduced their alcohol consumption, (because they were less inclined to visit public houses), one of the female survivors had started to drink heavily, often becoming intoxicated. Two men had become alcoholics and both attributed this as a response to the bombings.

When compared to the hospital casualty department 'attendees' group, the bombings survivors' incapacity to work (sickness) occurred in 59% of those affected by the blasts compared to the lower figure of 45% for attendees. The average number of days off work for the bomb survivors was 21 days, and just over 9 days for the comparison accident group.

Overall, the most important finding was that the Birmingham bomb survivors were much worse off symptomatically and socially than was anticipated. Deterioration in their family relationships and employment was often cited as being a direct result of the attacks on the two city centre pubs.

Psychological illness, often severe, was found in the majority of these lesser physically injured survivors interviewed for the study.

One person, who I knew socially, had been in one of the bombed pubs. She was there with her then boyfriend and afterwards they split up – every Thursday evening around the same time of the bombings and on the 21st day of each month she reported getting really upset. She was mentally creating time-related anniversaries of the incident.

Interestingly, one group of people who seemed to cope better after the Birmingham bombings, were employed by the former British Home Stores which was located on New Street right opposite the Tavern in the Town pub. Some had witnessed the aftermath of the bombings close to their place of work and were understandably affected by this.

The store provided those who returned with a room where they could retreat to and they didn't have to do any work. Occasionally I attended, often just providing a chat over tea and biscuits but it helped. Virtually all returned to work and suffered less in the way of long-term psychological problems. From this perspective it seemed that a prescription of a chat over tea and biscuits was more effective than a more formal debriefing.

Even half a century later, it is important for people to acknowledge the psychological impact of the bombings on families; friends; colleagues and wider communities. It is a big part of the history of Birmingham.

We are all tribal – tribal about being British, tribal about which city we live in and which part of that city. Then we have other tribes – football, work, groups of friends etc. After the bombings, a number of friendships, families and workplace connections were adversely affected. With the local Irish community they had arrived in an earlier period where they had to witness signs on properties for rent saying 'no dogs, Irish, blacks' and so on. They went on to become an important part of the fabric of the city, only to find themselves under attack again after the 1974 bombings by some of the wider community.

Over the years there has been reconciliation within the community, something which has happened with the passage of time. If there is a strong determination for reconciliation it can happen. My own extended family experienced the trauma of fleeing from Nazi Germany, with my father escaping to Britain from Vienna. He never talked about his escape from Austria or his internment on the Isle of Man as a potential enemy alien. Most of my family perished in the Holocaust. Did this experience of family trauma influence my choice of career?

Probably not and I think it comes from my own personality - I am innately nosey.

Today Birmingham is a big multi-cultural community – I live in Moseley, a vibrant cosmopolitan place with people from a wide range of cultural backgrounds.

I am delighted that the area is welcoming for all and we consider ourselves to be part of the Moseley tribe whatever our heritage.

Trauma can divide communities but it can also bring us together. As a psychiatrist I occasionally see the evil and bad in individuals but mostly I see ordinary people giving of their best.

** Aftermath Neurosis: Psychological Sequlae of Birmingham Bombings in victims not seriously injured. Andrew Sims; A White,:PJT Murphy Medical Science Law 1979. Vol 19-2 based on a study of 100 people.

After graduating in medicine and commencing psychiatry training Dr Alfred White became a lecturer for the University of Birmingham. He obtained a doctorate of medicine (MD) in 1980 having studied burns and other injuries and this led directly to a further study on the psychiatric effects of the Birmingham pub bombings.

JOURNALIST AND PHOTOGRAPHER STORIES

(By Enda Mullen)

Former Birmingham Post & Mail chief sports photographer Gerry Armes died at the age of 96 on September 10 this year.

Just a few weeks before, Gerry had spoken to Enda Mullen to tell of his recollections of the Birmingham pub bombings and crucially how the newspapers had been unable to cover the tragedy as comprehensively as might have been expected, due to a bitter industrial dispute at the time.

Gerry's family have expressed their wish that his words be included in the book - feeling that to do so would be most appropriate.

As well as being a respected photographer and a former National Union of Journalists (NUJ) Father of Chapel at the Post & Mail, Gerry was also a tireless fundraiser for the Journalists' Charity.

Gerry's Story

It was the greatest human tragedy to hit the Second City in the 20th century and a seismic news event. Yet newspaper coverage of the Birmingham pub bombings by the city's main print publisher was almost prevented by an industrial dispute that was going on at the time.

In the event there was some coverage but it was limited to say the least.

The bitter battle in November 1974 saw members of the National Union of Journalists (NUJ) at the Birmingham Post & Mail at loggerheads with the management in a pay dispute.

With an ongoing and seemingly unbreakable stalemate, NUJ members were holding continuous mandatory meetings - effectively strikes - which saw them stopping work at an agreed time for the remainder of the day.

Just such a meeting had been taking place when news of the pub bombings first filtered through and not surprisingly there was a keenness to return to work and cover the devastating events in the city.

A number of journalists at the Post & Mail at the time have shared their memories of what happened in the company's headquarters in Colmore Circus on the night of November 21st 1974 in the aftermath of the pub bombings

Gerry Armes, was the NUJ Father of Chapel (FOC) at the time, that role being the most senior elected union official who would lead negotiations with the management.

Gerry, was a photographer at the Birmingham publisher and has revealed how he and senior NUJ officials were prepared to call the action off in order to enable journalists to report on the bombings at the Mulberry Bush and Tavern in the Town.

Although not all the journalists at the Post & Mail were NUJ members, the majority were.

Gerry said: "We had a dispute with the management because there was a freeze on wages.

"We decided to have union meetings in the middle of the day - everybody went in the morning at about 11am and said we are now going on a mandatory meeting."

Gerry said that when the news of the explosions first came through there was a strong appreciation of just how devastating the pub bombings were and what a major news story it was.

He said: "The night of the bombings I offered we call it off, the managing director refused."

From the union perspective Gerry said they thought that was it, but in an unexpected about turn just a few hours later the boot was on the other foot when the managing director came to the union to ask whether they would go back to work. However, any mood of conciliation that prevailed previously had changed.

"He came to us and said would we call the meeting off," said Gerry. "I said no, four or five hours ago I offered to you to call it off and you refused.

"I said you make me sick and walked out."

Gerry recalls the coverage, which was somewhat cobbled together by the available staff that evening and management, was adequate rather than incisive and in-depth.

He said that the limited staff resources meant they managed to just about cover the bombings as best as they could but other news was sacrificed.

While some might have thought that was indicative of the fact there was only one story in town, any regional newspaper of the time would still have endeavoured to offer coverage of other things happening in the city that day.

As it turned out, the dispute did not go on much longer - Gerry can't be certain but said he thinks it came to an end within a couple of days.

In all the toings and froings of what must have been a dramatic evening at the Post & Mail's Colmore Circus offices, was FOC Gerry Armes' first offer to call off the industrial action one that he felt he could sell to union members?

While he acknowledges that some of his memories have been dulled over time he sums up the position succinctly by saying: "We were just being bloody awkward."

Recollections from former Birmingham journalists

There can be no disputing the fact the Post & Mail's coverage of the immediate aftermath of the pub bombings was severely hampered, as other journalists at the time confirm.

Former journalists Bob Haywood and Barry Phillips recently shared their recollections, via the Birmingham Press Club, on why many of the city's reporters were unable to cover what was probably Birmingham's biggest news event of the last century.

They offer further fascinating insight into the bitter ongoing industrial dispute and its effect on coverage of the pub bombings. While Bob's recollections do not reflect any sense of a compromise, Barry does recall senior members of the union chapel approaching the management with an offer to at least suspend the industrial action.

Clearly and perhaps not surprisingly there was some division among the union membership and as Bob Haywood recalls some members did break ranks and go back to work.

Their recollections, which were published earlier this year in the Birmingham Press Club newsletter, are below.

Bob Haywood:

Former Birmingham Evening Mail journalist Bob Haywood is also an ex-news editor of the Mail's sister-publication, the Sunday Mercury. He started his career as a trainee reporter with the Smethwick Telephone, later going on to being Trinity Mirror's Reporter of the Year in 1999 and twice winning the accolade of BT Midlands Journalist of the Year.

"On the night of 21st November 1974, bombs ripped through The Tavern in the Town and The Mulberry Bush pubs in Birmingham city centre, killing 21 people and maiming more than 200.

It was the worst IRA outrage on the British mainland in the 20 years of The Troubles.

With the 50th anniversary of the massacre looming, much will be written yet again about this day of infamy.

But anyone looking back in the files of the Birmingham newspapers at the time will probably be surprised at the sketchy coverage in the immediate aftermath.

This is because the copy was written – and the photographs taken – by just a few staff journalists, bulked out by coverage from news agencies such as the Press Association.

In those days, the Birmingham Post & Mail Ltd – publishers of the Birmingham Evening Mail, The Birmingham Post and the Sunday Mercury – employed about 250 journalists.

Most of them worked at Post & Mail House in Colmore Circus, but others were based all across the West Midlands in district offices.

So why was the pub bombings coverage at the time so sparse?

Well, at the time, almost all of the editorial staff were effectively on strike – more coyly 'attending a continuous mandatory meeting' of the Post & Mail chapel of the National Union of Journalists (NUJ).

By chance, dozens of the chapel members were actually in the Post & Mail building . . . but not in the newsroom.

They were two floors up in the The Quiet Room where (in more normal times) staff could go during their shift breaks to read a paper or book in a comfy chair.

The room had no TV or radio or landline phone, and even whispering was frowned on.

But during this era of industrial relations turbulence, The Quiet Room was an arena of noisy debate and discussion . . . for hours on end!

At the time, I was a firebrand member of the NUJ chapel committee so it was often me making most of the noise.

Because we were all jammed into The Quiet Room with no contact with the outside world (no mobile phones in those days, of course) we knew nothing of the pub bombs going off until the city centre was suddenly engulfed in a cacophony of sirens from police cars, fire engines and ambulances rushing to the stricken pubs.

Soon, a messenger from the skeletal news desk tapped on the door and passed on the message: "There have been two bombs. It looks really bad."

The go-between later returned at quick intervals, saying:

"There are fatalities", then "The death toll is five", then "Ten", then "Twenty".

The duty editors asked for a pow-wow and the chapel

committee agreed. But no deal could be hammered out on a return to work - solely to cover the bombings.

After the chapel negotiators trooped back to The Quiet Room to break the 'no deal' news to members, a vote was taken. It was overwhelmingly against calling off the meeting. A handful of members voted to go back – and walked out of the room, very vocally or in silence.

In both factions, NUJ members were stunned – some in tears as their loyalties and consciences were being ripped apart.

Those NUJ members who walked out joined the few Birmingham Post editors and other editorial staff who were either in the rival Institute of Journalists (IoJ), or in neither union, and still working in the newsroom and naturally struggling to get editions out.

If a back-to-work deal could have been done, the Post & Mail would have had (by pure chance) dozens of its seasoned reporters and photographers ready to dash out to cover the bombings, just five minutes' walk away.

Looking back 50 years, this all seems a very odd, even perverse, standoff. But these were febrile times in provincial journalism with the NUJ and newspaper companies, locally and nationally, virtually in a state of perpetual war.

Circulations were sky high – and so were profits – but rank-and-file journalists felt they were under-valued and badly underpaid. So goodwill was a very rare commodity. On the night of the Birmingham pub bombings, principle – or obstinacy if you wish – ruled in the end."

Barry Phillips

Barry had worked on five publications in Birmingham and Solihull by 1974 when he worked for the Birmingham Evening Mail.

"Minutes before the explosions the newspaper received a warning of the impending attacks from an IRA associate who used the code Double X to phone the switchboard that bombs had been planted and to tell the police.

The call, intended to give a 30-minute warning, came too late, however, because the first phone box chosen for the call was out of order.

Senior members of the NUJ chapel approached management within minutes of the enormity of the explosions being realised and offered to suspend the strike. Instead, executives of the various city titles decided they would step into the shoes of the absentee foot-slogging scribes and with the help of non-union writers, unaffiliated freelances, national news agencies and the London dailies who sent teams to cover the story, limited editions were compiled by the Birmingham news desk and printed to convey the news across the region.

Few readers noticed the lack of some other regular content, omitted because in concentrating on the huge drama on their doorstep, the makeshift editorial team had neither resources nor space for little else."

Recollections from the late photographer MJ Niels McGuinness

Given journalists and photographers who were union members at the Birmingham Post & Mail were on strike at the time, the photographs taken by freelance press photographer the late MJ

Niels McGuinness were in high demand.

He was on the scene at the Mulberry Bush not long after the first bomb had gone off and described the experience as "a night I shall never forget" when reflecting on that evening later in his life.

He said: "Someone said a bomb had gone off in New Street - I couldn't believe it. So I sped like hell towards the city centre.

"I arrived at the Rotunda within minutes of the explosions. It was a scene reminiscent of a newsreel from the Blitz. Broken plate glass windows littered the surrounding streets - people were screaming and running in all directions from the devastation caused by the bombs, which exploded within minutes.

"I took a picture of fireman Ralph Dawson with a young lad carrying bodies in red canvas sheets."

Niels recalled entering the Mulberry Bush through a large plate glass window, which had once been there but had been "smashed to smithereens" and how he "tread discreetly amongst the bodies, rubble, and broken furniture" unable to find anyone who might possibly still be alive.

He also recalled the grim sight of a person who had been flung by the force of the explosion through a side window onto the side passage, landing face down.

He said: "By the time I raised my camera to focus, two firemen threw a blanket over the body and quickly carried it away."

One of the firemen told Niels of the second bomb at the Tavern in the Town nearby.

Given the chaos in the city in the aftermath of the bombs exploding, Niels told how it was hard to hire a taxi - due in part to the fact many taxi drivers had stepped in to help ferry victims to hospital.

He managed to persuade one taxi driver to deliver the films containing the photographs he had taken directly to Fleet Street.

Pictures were released to all national newspapers, the provincial press and television newsrooms during the early hours of the following morning.

Another abiding memory of Niels' that evening was of one of the victims, Carl Bacon from Kings Norton, being discharged from hospital, where staff and volunteers had been working flat out to treat the wounded.

Niels said: "I took his picture walking off in the night, resembling The Invisible Man. His entire head was wrapped in bandages."

Niels' work was far from over though, he had to race to the Coventry Evening Telegraph to process pictures that could be wired to Fleet Street for when the morning shift arrived.

Then at dawn he was instructed to take pictures of Roy Jenkins, the Home Secretary and MP for Stechford, visiting the scene of the devastation, while more pictures were required of the Duke of Edinburgh visiting victims in hospital.

Peter Kennedy

The late Peter Kennedy, a BBC journalist at the time, was the first reporter on the scene at the Mulberry Bush, something which came about by chance.

Peter had been at New Street railway station waiting to catch a train when he heard a huge explosion - the first of the two bombs go off at the packed pub at the foot of the Rotunda.

His journalistic reflexes kicked in immediately and he raced the short distance from the platform to the Mulberry Bush, where a scene of horror and devastation greeted him.

Peter made contact with the news desk at the BBC in Birmingham, phoning in the first on the spot news reports related to the pub bombings.

Many decades on Peter still spoke of that evening with colleagues and anyone who was interested, myself included.

A jovial ebullient and at times cynical fellow, very much in the old school of the journalistic profession, he was always happy to speak of the experience.

However it was clear even many years on that it was one which had been profoundly shocking and something which continued to have a deep impact on him.

Campaigning local journalism

Although coverage of the pub bombings by the Birmingham Post & Mail was limited, due to strike action by journalists and photographers at the time, the Birmingham Mail has played a prominent role in campaigning for justice for the victims and their families since then.

The most recent recognition of this was in June 2020, when the Mail won the Campaign of the Year accolade at the Regional Press Awards.

The awards honour Britain's best journalism and judges praised the Mail's successful support of the families of the victims of the pub bombings.

Is was the second time the Mail won the Campaign of the Year award for its support of the families, also picking up the title in

2017.

The Mail's campaign - seeking justice for those who died in the pub bombings and their families - has been spearheaded in recent years by content editor Andy Richards.

The 2020 award recognised the pivotal role of the Mail in the resumption of inquests into the 21 killed in the atrocity.

The Mail also continued to press for the identities of the suspected bombers to be revealed, something which continued as reporters attended every day of the 29-day inquest hearing, which opened on February 25 2019.

Although the coroner had ruled the naming of the suspected bombers outside the scope of the inquests, names were heard during evidence.

It was Andy Richards who identified a legal loophole which enabled the inquests to go ahead. While trawling legal documents and archive news reports, he realised that although the inquests had been opened after the tragedy, they were never completed. This was because police immediately arrested the Birmingham Six, who were later cleared of the crime.

It was judged that there was then no need for the inquests to continue but, crucially, they were never closed.

Working with lawyers, and the Justice4the21 campaign group formed by Julie and Brian Hambleton – whose sister Maxine was among those who died in the bombings – Andy Richards first brought the loophole to the attention of the authorities, and then campaigned relentlessly for the inquests to be resumed.

The families, for whom the Mail has fought since 1974, finally began to get some longstanding questions answered, including the naming of the bombers, the police staff shortages on the night the bombers struck, and the emergency services shortcomings and inadequate equipment supply.

The final inquest conclusion was that the 21 people who died were unlawfully killed.

The judges of the 2020 Regional Press Awards said: "This is a campaign that made a difference thanks to the dogged determination of Andy Richards, who refused to cave in even when faced with massive official resistance to his pursuit for justice.

"This long-running campaign has finally seen some justice for the victims' families – as well as revealed names and evidence that has been suppressed over the years."

CARL CHINN'S STORY

(In conversation with Maggie Fogarty)

It isn't often that you meet one of your history writing heroes and I was delighted when Professor Carl Chinn agreed to share his own thoughts and reflections for this commemorative book.

Over the years in my role as a TV producer we have had occasional phone chats but this meeting is our first 'in person' one. Carl is exactly how I expect him to be – a straight talking no-nonsense proud Brummie – with an extensive expert knowledge of Birmingham local history. He also has a great talent for story-telling and explaining things simply without being simplistic.

We start with Carl's memories of the night of the bombings. He was at school at the time studying for A levels but would often go out to Birmingham night clubs like the Locarno, Top Rank and Rebecca's.

'I would go into town mainly at the weekend but occasionally in the week. That Thursday night I stayed in and was at home with mom and dad. My younger brother, our kid, should have gone to town that night but didn't go for various reasons.'

'I remember the news flashes started coming up on the TV and went on throughout the evening. It wasn't like today when you have 24/7 news – in those days when a news flash came up on the TV you stopped what you were doing.'

Carl adds that his only previous memory of news flashes was as a young child, after President Kennedy had been shot in 1963 and seeing his mom and aunt crying.

'When we saw those news flashes on the night of the 1974 bombings we knew it was serious. Then we started to worry. Were there any friends of ours there? Thank God our kid had stayed home that night. There were no mobile phones then and many people didn't have phones in their houses. They had to go out to use public phone boxes.'

Carl says that as the evening wore on they realised it was a horrendous situation, waking up early the next day to find out even more horrific news about the extent of the deaths and injuries.

'We knew what was going on in Northern Ireland, knew how bad things were, how the Catholics had been discriminated against with atrocities on both sides including the IRA. I was always interested in politics and growing up with lots of Birmingham Irish people, I understood some Irish history.'

Carl's parents had good friends in Dublin and the family used to go and visit them from time to time. As a family of bookmakers Carl was also helping out at that time with the family businesses in Sparkbrook, on the Ladypool Road, Stoney Lane and Highgate Road. A lot of the customers were local Irish men. He remembers that they were generous men – one gave him a £1 after he won a big amount, which for the then 16 year old was a lot of money.

'Before the bombings I remember my mom and dad telling us to be careful if we went out at night, to check if there were any suspicious packages lying around but the attacks on the pubs changed everything. We had to be more alert. There had been doormen at clubs like the Locarno and Top Rank checking people over to see if they were smartly dressed but they weren't looking for explosives. The pub bombings changed all that and Birmingham became a place where people were more fearful.'

I tell Carl about my own memory of my mum saying that she felt ashamed to be Irish the next day and he remembers only too well the devastating effects on the Birmingham Irish community which he was a part of and loved.

'At the time I had many Irish friends. We played football over the Rec, Sarehole Park, with the McGonigles, the Fagans, lots of lads I grew up with and played football with. My mom's grandmother was half Irish and when I married my Irish wife Kay from Dublin, we sang Irish songs at our wedding.'

Through his work at the family betting shops, Carl got to know a lot of groups of older Irish men. Most of them wouldn't talk about the pub bombings afterwards because it was too hurtful. Like my own mum they felt ashamed about what had happened in the city that they had made home.

'One mate – Billy Hughes – worked at the Rover car factory. When he went into work the next day he said that he understood the anger of the English workers and that as a Dubliner he said he was ashamed to be Irish.'

He recalls Billy saying: 'Carl they have said they are doing it in our name but they are not'.

Carl adds that when the Longbridge and other factory workers went on anti-Irish marches to protest, it was an outpouring of anger and that is probably what the IRA wanted – to split the community.

'Just two years after the bombings I was going into Irish pubs, drank with local Irish men and for the majority things had calmed down by then. I do remember there was a big march by Sinn Fein in the city a few years after the bombings and a lot of us went up there to protest – not to be anti-Irish but just to protest that they were marching in our city where such horrors had taken place. I would have done the same if the UDA had turned up.'

Carl met his Irish wife in 1977 and they married the following year. He says that Kay never faced any anti-Irish prejudice in the city. When her mom and dad came over to visit the newly married couple in 1979, they took them to a working-class Royal British Legion club in Birmingham. Kay's dad was worried, checking if it was OK for them to go in there after the Birmingham bombings. Carl assured then it would be fine and they had a great night out.

'It was the aftershock of the bombings that led to the backlash from some Birmingham people against the local Irish community – not the majority of local people. After the bombings there would be collections at some Irish pubs from IRA sympathisers especially around the anniversary of the Easter Rising. This annoyed some of the local Irish people – it was a shared space they had with local Birmingham people and was seen as our combined space. I went to Aston Villa matches with my friend Billy from Dublin, a Catholic, along with a Protestant friend from East Belfast, and another Catholic from Roscommon. We were all good mates and didn't need IRA supporters coming into our space and shaking tins. What they didn't realise back then is that there were not just Irish drinking in those pubs, there were English as well.'

Over the years Carl has written about the pub bombings for the Birmingham local press, often highlighting the role played by ordinary people that night, like the taxi drivers who ferried people to hospitals when the ambulances struggled to cope.

Also firefighters and other frontline workers who all pulled together that night.

I tell Carl that as well as being a first class social historian, he is a good journalist with a great way of story-telling. I also admire the way he can write simply without being 'simplistic' – the mark of a good journalist.

While he doesn't agree that he is journalist, he does accept my compliment about writing in a straightforward way, adding that he always puts ordinary people at the heart of his stories.

'Although my family were better off as bookies, my mom was proud of the fact that she came from a family who lived in back-to-back houses in Aston before moving into council houses. My nan moved from her back-to-back in Aston into a maisonette in Nechells. Growing up I would always listen to stories from my mom and dad, my nan and generations of family going back to Victorian times.'

Reflecting on the 50 years since the 1974 bombings, Carl alludes to the fact that at times in our chat we have both found ourselves in tears.

He says: 'We got a bit upset talking today and if we are both like that 50 years on when we weren't personally involved, how traumatic is it for the survivors, the people who lost loved ones, those who witnessed things that night, the Irish people who suffered attacks and discrimination as well as having some of their own community killed in the bombings too? How hard is it for them?'

Carl gets tearful again when he recalls hosting a big event at Birmingham Town Hall in 2014 for the 40th anniversary of the bombings.

'I said that while it was all of the people of Birmingham affected by the bombings, let's not forget the two Irish brothers who also died that evening. A family in the circle shouted out "thank you"...'

Carl adds that it is also important to remember that there were two young black men, 'Tommy' Marsh and Paul Davies, both killed as they walked in front of the Mulberry Bush pub.

'The after effects are still there 50 years on, the wounds still there because to date nobody has been held accountable for the bombings.'

Carl supports the call for a full public inquiry campaigned for by the Justice4the21 group and is critical of both local and national politicians across the political parties for not getting behind this enough.

'It's as if the people of Birmingham do not matter, the lives lost that night are not worthy of an inquiry like the one the Hillsborough families fought for and other campaign groups.'

At the same time he pays tribute to the Birmingham Irish Association and its Chief Executive Maurice Malone who along with the families of the 21 people killed have created the striking metal tree memorial at the gateway to Grand Central (New Street) station.

As we come to the end of our chat Carl adds:

'As I see it the people who died that night have had more support, care and consideration from the people of Ireland represented by their President and the Irish of Birmingham. As a proud Brummie with Irish links I just want to say thank you for what they have done.'

Professor Carl Chinn MBE DL Ph.D. F.Birm.Soc. is a social historian with a national profile, writer, teacher, and public speaker.

Thanks to:

All of the commemorative book contributors for sharing their stories and experiences from that awful time half a century ago. You have left a slice of personal history and testimony for future generations.

To Andrew Sparke at APS books for the cover design using a photo by the late press photographer MJ Niels McGuinness, with permission for use given by his wife Gill McGuinness and granddaughter Louisa.

To survivor Maureen Mitchell for her additional book advice and to fellow journalist Enda Mullen.

To Professor Gavin Schaffer for the book foreword.

To The Irish Post newspaper for allowing us to reprint the words of the late Birmingham and Irish community photojournalist, Brendan Farrell.

To Pat Wright, Maria Cleary and Maggie Roche who have helped with my TV projects over the years and who gave some good early advice on the book project..

To my husband Paul for all his support and hard work in formatting the book contributions.

To all involved in creating the poignant tree memorial near the entrance to Grand Central (New Street) station, including the Birmingham Irish Association and the families of the victims.

In Memoriam…..

Michael William Beasley

Lynn Jane Bennett

Stanley James Bodman

James Frederick Caddick

Thomas Frederick Chaytor

James Goodlett Craig

Paul Anthony Davies

Jane Elizabeth Davis

Charles Harper Grey

Maxine Hambleton

Anne Hayes

John Clifford Jones

Neil Robert 'Tommy' Marsh

Marilyn Paula Nash

Pamela Joan Palmer

Desmond William Reilly

Eugene Thomas Reilly

Maureen Anne Roberts

John Rowlands

Trevor George Thrupp

Stephen John Whalley

To all those survivors and others whose lives were impacted by the Birmingham bombings on November 21st 1974

About the Writers

Maggie Fogarty is a senior award winning television producer/journalist and has made UK television programmes for the BBC, ITV, Channel 4 and Channel 5. She has also written for a number of national newspapers and magazines covering social affairs stories. Maggie helped to set up the BASW UK Journalism Awards and has been a member of the judging team.

Enda Mullen is a freelance journalist and writer who has worked in the regional press for 28 years.

During that time he was a news, business and motoring writer for several newspapers, including the Birmingham Post & Mail and the Coventry Telegraph - as well as writing for national titles such as the Mirror and Daily Record.

Printed in Great Britain
by Amazon

c7e6e14c-b446-47e8-9169-6d32b98cfc44R01